— AN EXPONENTIAL RESOURCE —

TOGETHER WITH FAMILY

FLOURISHING IN A **LEVEL FIVE** MARRIAGE

LARRY & DEB WALKEMEYER

≡XPONENTIAL

EXPONENTIAL

Together with Family: Flourishing in a Level Five Marriage
Copyright © 2017 by Larry and Deb Walkemeyer

Exponential is a growing movement of activists committed to the multiplication of healthy new churches. Exponential Resources spotlights actionable principles, ideas and solutions for the accelerated multiplication of healthy, reproducing faith communities. For more information, visit exponential.org

All rights reserved. No part of this book, including icons and images, may be reproduced in any manner without prior written permission from copyright holder, except where noted in the text and in the case of brief quotations embodied in critical articles and reviews.

This book is manufactured in the United States.

Unless otherwise indicated, all Scripture quotations are taken from the Holy Bible, New International Version, copyright ©1973, 1978, 1984, 2011 by International Bible Society. All emphases in Scripture quotations have been added by the author.

Scripture quotations marked (TLB) are taken from The Living Bible copyright © 1971. Used by permission of Tyndale House Publishers, Inc., Carol Stream, Illinois 60188. All rights reserved.

Scriptures marked *The Message* are taken from THE MESSAGE, copyright © 1993, 1994, 1995, 1996, 2000, 2001, 2002 by Eugene H. Peterson. Used by permission of NavPress. All rights reserved. Represented by Tyndale House Publishers, Inc.

Scriptures marked GW are taken from GOD'S WORD® copyright© 1995 by God's Word to the Nations. All rights reserved.

Scriptures marked NAS are taken from the *New American Standard* (1960, 1962, 1963, 1968, 1971, 1972,1973, 1975, 1977, 1995 by The Lockman Foundation. All rights reserved. Used by permission.

Scriptures marked NLT are taken from the New Living Translation Copyright ©1996, 2004, 2007. Used by permission of Tyndale House Publishers, Inc., Carol Stream, Illinois 60188.

ISBN: 978-1-62424-045-4 (ebook)
ISBN: 978-1-62424-049-2 (print)

Edited by Lindy Lowry & Jan Greggo

Foreword by Dave and Sue Ferguson

Cover and interior design by Harrington Interactive Media

Inside

Foreword *by Dave and Sue Ferguson* 11

Introduction 13

Chapter 1
The Ministry Marriage 21

Chapter 2
Five Levels of Marriage: Which One Are You? 29

Chapter 3
Habit 1 / The Humility You Practice 57

Chapter 4
Habit 2 / Spiritually Engaged 73

Chapter 5
Habit 3 / The Honor You Show 89

Chapter 6
Habit 4 / The Passion You Inspire 103

Chapter 7
Habit 5 / Vision Alignment 119

Chapter 8
By God's Grace for God's Purpose 137

Endnotes 145

About the Authors 147

With Thanks to . . .

Exponential

Thank you, Todd Wilson, for your priority on this crucial topic, your wisdom, and for being our friend. Lindy Lowry, we are grateful to have an editor we can totally trust because of your phenomenal expertise combined with your huge heart. Bill Couchenour, Terri Saliba, Brooks Hamon, Anna Wilson, and Mariah Wilson, thanks for being the team behind the scenes to make it all happen. We are honored to serve alongside you and admire you.

Light & Life Christian Fellowship

You are our spiritual family who has grown with us on this grand adventure since 1991. Your love and support for our marriage has helped us build the relationship we write about here. Thank you for your prayers and for the sabbatical we used to write this book. We love you immensely.

The Free Methodist Church in Southern California

Thank you for your support for us. You have encouraged us to give attention to both our marriage and ministry and have supported us on this writing sabbatical, and we are grateful.

To the Married Couples Who Have Blessed Us and Invested in Us:

We have seen Christ in your marriages, and you have imparted Christ to our marriage. Thanks to Dwight and Shelley Pauls (our best friends for thirty-five years), Mark and Brenda Williams, JR and Kim Rushik, Carol and Dave Duberowski, Mark and Terri McGrath, Tom and Holli Applegate, Travis and Katie Wade, Bob and Susan Combs, Denny and Cheryl Wayman, Gary and Marty Enniss, and many others.

To Our Children:

Lindsey, TJ, and Anjelica, thanks for being the kind of kids who love Jesus and make us look like we knew what we were doing. You have supported our marriage in so many valuable ways. We love you to the moon and back.

exponential.org

EXPONENTIAL

RESOURCING CHURCH PLANTERS

- 90+ eBooks
- Largest annual church planting conference in the world (Exponential Global Event in Orlando)
- Regional Conferences - Boise, DC, Southern CA, Bay Area CA, Chicago, Houston and New York City
- Exponential Español (spoken in Spanish)
- 200+ Roundtables on Topics like Church Multiplication, Mobilization, Church Planting, Emotionally Healthy Leaders, The Future of the Church, and More
- Exponential HUB - Free Digital Platform offering content & conversation (multiplication.org/HUB)
- FREE Online Multiplication & Mobilization Assessments
- FREE Online Multiplication & Mobilization Courses
- Conference content available via Digital Access Pass (Training Videos)
- Weekly Newsletter
- 1000+ Hours of Free Audio Training
- 100s of Hours of Free Video Training
- Free Podcast Interviews

exponential.org

Twitter.com/churchplanting
Facebook.com/churchplanting
Instagram.com/church_planting

Foreword

Uplifting! In a word, what you are about to read is very uplifting! If you want to move a struggling marriage to a good marriage or move a good marriage to a great marriage, *Together with Family* is a terrific book to show you how to lift your most important relationship up a level. Larry & Deb Walkemeyer draw on over 40 years of marriage experience to teach all of us about the 5 different levels of marriage and how we can take our marriages up a notch. *Together with Family* is the kind of book that will give you clear guidance on how to lift your marriage from level 1 marriage based on consumerism to a level 5 marriage based on communion. We found the Walkemeyer's writing uplifting in the following three ways:

- Uplifting Wisdom. Every word of *Together with Family* is grounded in Scripture as the truth source. When you combine God's Word and the Walkemeyer's experience, you get wisdom. This is the kind of wisdom that every young couple should take advantage of and apply immediately.
- Uplifting Application. *Together with Family* is not just theory, theology, or philosophy; it is pain-staking practical. It offers five habits for taking your marriage up a level and then gives you a whole chapter on each of the practices. And just to make sure this is not a book you only read, but you apply, they end each of the chapters on habits with a self-assessment.
- Uplifting Stories. *Together with Family* is filled with stories. Some of the stories are personal stories from the authors' lives; other stories are from the many people they have served and ministered to over the years. The stories remind you that what you are reading will work in your marriage.

A favorite movie of ours is "UP." If you saw it, you remember that it has one of the most moving and romantic opening five minutes of any movie ever! We had barely found our seats and had only a couple handfuls of popcorn, and through Pixar magic they had us in tears. Remember the story of "UP"? Carl and Ellie meant to go to Paradise Falls. They really wanted to go to Paradise Falls. But life happened and now Ellie is gone. They never made it there.

The reason "UP" moved us is because that's so often how it goes, isn't it? We want certain things to be true of our marriage and long for certain things to be a part of our marriage, but stuff happens, and before we know it, it's too late and we're left with regret. We never make it to Paradise Falls. Don't waste another day longing and dreaming about your "Paradise Falls." Do you want to take your marriage up a level? Read *Together with Family*. It's uplifting!

—Dave & Sue Ferguson
Community Christian Church | NewThing

Introduction

Flourish: to grow or develop in a healthy or vigorous way, especially as the result of a particularly favorable environment.

Level 0. Level zero is what it felt like in 1977 when our pre-marriage counselor made the declaration: "I would suggest that you two do not get married. You are both such strong personalities you will either kill each other or change the world."

Good news! We are married, we are both still alive, and we believe we have had some impact on our small part of the world. On top of that, we have had a journey of outrageous joy over the last nearly forty years of marriage. Yes, there have been moments we've wanted to strangle each other. Other times we have wept in each other's arms. We've been opposed and oppressed by the evil one. We have survived cancer, living on welfare, church splits, church crashes, near-marital separation, near-death experiences, ministry failures, betrayals, and much more. But God has been dynamically faithful, day after day.

As we step into our fortieth year of marriage, we love living in the life we have built and are praying that God gives us forty more years together. For all those years, plus a year of dating, we've been deeply engaged in ministry. As the years have gone by, we have studied our marriage and hundreds of other marriages to gain some insights we're sharing with leaders like you in this book.

Level 5 Churches Require Level 5 Marriages

Over the past four years, Deb and I have been inspired and convicted through our participation in the work of Exponential. We believe Exponential's recent work on the five levels of church multiplication is a crucial prophetic word for the Church today. The research they have provided and fully explored in the book *Becoming a Level 5 Multiplying Church* sparked the thinking for this marriage book.[1]

Exponential's five church profiles (Level 1: Declining; Level 2: Plateaued; Level 3: Growing; Level 4: Reproducing; and Level 5: Multiplying) catalyzed our ideas on the quality or stages of the marriages we have observed. We began to understand the connection between the five levels of churches and the five levels of marriages. With some rare exceptions, churches tend to reflect the quality or stage of the lead pastor's marriage. We're confident in saying that if a couple aspires to lead a Level 5 church, they probably will not succeed unless they build a Level 5 marriage. In fact, we'll go so far to say it's a fallacy to think you can build a Level 5 multiplying church while ignoring your marriage.

Level 5 churches require hero-making Level 5 leaders with Level 5 marriages. When you develop a healthy marriage and work to see it multiply into other healthy marriages that are learning from yours, you're more readily positioned to multiply churches, as well. We encourage couples to read *Becoming a Level 5 Multiplying Church* and Exponential's book, *Multipliers: Leading Beyond Addition,* as companion books to this one. Also, Exponential has a huge library of other free eBooks and resources that complement the content in this book.

From Level 1 to Level 5 Marriage

Deb and I believe (and have experienced firsthand) that any marriage can travel from its current level to a Level 5 marriage. We're the first to say the journey isn't easy—far from it. A Level 5 marriage requires each of you to learn, grow, and rely on the Holy Spirit. Specifically, it relies on practicing the five vital habits we identify and explore in this book.

We want to be transparent and tell you that our marriage has not arrived. We are "with you" on this upward climb. Deb and I have worked hard on our marriage, and (thanks be to God!) most days our marriage is a Level 4 (more about the specific levels in the next chapter). Increasingly, it's a Level 5. We are growing. We have discovered that every effort is worth it. The higher we climb, the more love and joy we share in our marriage *and* the more effective we are in building the Kingdom together. Also, the best gift you can give to your family is a great marriage.

While these five levels of marriage aren't rooted in empirical research, they are the product of our own education and experiences. Deb is a licensed marriage and family therapist and for nine years, her emphasis has been ministry couples. After joining our Light & Life church staff as co-pastor, she continued to mentor pastors and spouses. Three years ago In 2014, Deb received her Doctor of Ministry in Church Leadership from Fuller Seminary. I'm not exaggerating when I say that Deb has seen it all in marriages!

I, too, have observed a lot in my various experiences in youth ministries, missions work, conference speaking, church planting, denominational oversight and twenty-six years as lead pastor of Light & Life. In fact, what I was seeing in married couples led me to pursue my ministry doctorate and emphasis in spiritual formation and leadership. Through my experience, I discovered that the health of a pastor's/leader's marriage nearly always reveals the health of their soul and also impacts the health of their church or ministry.

In this book, like most areas of our marriage, Deb is more the brains, and I am more the mouth. Deb has the spiritual gift of wisdom while I have a preaching gift. She instructs people; I inspire them. We're a great combo! While I'm the one putting most of the words on the page, Deb has informed every aspect of the truths we share here.

Many years ago, I recall a speaker (whose name I have since forgotten) declare, "Marriage is two becoming one. This starts as an event but happens as a journey. The question is, 'How *one* do you want your marriage to be?'" We believe this is the priority question for you as a couple: *What level of "oneness" are you working toward in your marriage?* Deb and I have determined that we want our marriage to be as "one" as it can be, not just for our sake, but especially for the sake of the Kingdom.

The concept of "oneness" is found throughout the New Testament, especially in the "One" prayer of Jesus in John 17. Praying before his crucifixion, Jesus prayed that his disciples would become one as he and the Father are one, and that their unity would be a testimony to his Lordship. After spending three and a half years with such a diverse, often competitive, group of men, Jesus knew only the life-changing power of the Holy Spirit could pull off such a miracle! For this movement of God to really take off, it required a supernatural unity that the world had never witnessed. With the empowerment of the Spirit given at Pentecost this unity happened, though certainly not without snags.

Unity in the church is still vital for effective ministry and cannot be attained without the collaboration of all. When it comes to ministry marriages, this same unity is critical when working side by side in Kingdom work. Unfortunately, we have neglected the importance of unity, of "oneness", when it comes to our effectiveness. So often we work in our individual silos, hoping to achieve important things for God, but our partner and/or our kids, get left behind. Knowing this, the Exponential team has created resources to help ministers grow in this area. A "Great Collaboration" in our marriages and family is critical to understand because we are better together!

This "Great Collaboration" in John 17 often gets sidestepped by ministers for the misplaced value on one—the individual person working in his or her isolated bubbles. But as Dave Ferguson writes, "Jesus offers us a vision of a 'Together' church that prioritizes relationships (friendships, marriage & family) and community (teamwork, partnerships and networks) as the way to be and do God's mission." Growing a Level 5 marriage is about moving from individuals in a ministry marriage surviving life, to becoming a couple and family truly committed to serving the mission TOGETHER.

We realize some of you are starting from a very tough place. Perhaps your marriage is hanging by a thread or seems hopeless. Maybe you'd describe it as "ho-hum," "neglected," or "as stale as three-year-old crackers." You might have a "good-enough" marriage and think you can coast the rest of the way. Or you may be having lots of fun in your marriage, but you realize or sense that it's lacking significant Kingdom impact.

We also know that only you can change you. Some anonymous wise person (not sure of this name either) once said, "Women marry men thinking their man will change. Men marry women thinking their woman will never change. Both are wrong." You may have a spouse who's stuck and unwilling to read and apply the insights and practical teaching we share. Don't let that reality stop you from getting a vision for your marriage and starting to practice these habits on your own. We have seen dead and buried marriages resurrected by the power of Jesus working with the initial efforts of one of the spouses.

Our Approach

As Deb and I began to write, we intentionally set out to make sure we didn't wind up with a traditional "how-to" marriage book. Our experiences have shown us that when we teach marriage skills and principles, they have limited value unless the "heart habits" change. If the hearts of the husband and wife are not transformed by the power of the Holy Spirit, the skills produce little lasting effect in the marriage. To that end, we have sought to go to the root of marriage problems and marriage potential.

We have identified five vital "heart habits" and have strived to take these habits out of the theoretical and give them practical handles. These words are meant to "become flesh," designed to be incarnated each day in the mundane and chaotic moments of real life. Our own marriage has been a laboratory for these habits and handles. We have discovered that when we approach our marriage from a spiritual, attitudinal posture but also demand tangible expressions for these mindsets, then real and lasting growth happens.

We want to help you get the most from this book, so we have a few suggestions for how to read it. If you're a ministry couple (one or both of you are in vocational ministry), you definitely want to pay close attention to chapter 1 in which we focus on the unique dynamics of ministry marriages. If yours isn't a ministry marriage, we suggest you skip to chapter 2 and begin the assessment process by exploring the characteristics of the five levels of marriage we've identified. We recommend reading chapter 2 individually and then coming together to discuss what you think your current marriage level is.

Chapters 3-7 discuss each of the five habits vital for growing your marriage to Level 5.

At the end of each chapter, we've included ten assessment statements to help you evaluate your marriage on a scale of 1 to 5. If you choose, you can add up the number for each of your answers and then divide that number by fifty to get an idea of the level your marriage is currently experiencing. If you do this, we encourage you to complete the assessment for each chapter individually and then come together to discuss your individual scores.

INTRODUCTION

Wherever your marriage is today, we can say without a doubt that God has more for it! As the title of this book reflects, God wants your marriage to flourish—to grow and develop in a healthy, vigorous way because you're in a particularly favorable environment. He wants you to flourish both in your marriage and as individuals. In fact, *His dream for your marriage is bigger and better than your dream for it.* Do you believe that? Deep down, do you think God has something powerful and Kingdom-building for this union you entered into the day you stared into each other's eyes and intentionally said your vows?

Trust us. Your marriage can be significantly better a year from today. You can be flourishing. The life-giving truth is that *God is more committed to your marriage than you are.* His power is more available for your marriage than you have yet imagined or accessed. Have faith in His plan and power! Our prayer is this book would be one notable tool God uses to move your marriage forward, ultimately to Level 5. We are writing with the vision that your marriage can be more fulfilling for you and more fruitful for the Kingdom.

Important Note:

One of the pressing discussions in the American Church today is the role of women in ministry. While this issue is quite important to us, we have endeavored to write in a way that rises above the divisiveness of this debate. We have deliberately attempted to share in a way that both our complementarian and egalitarian friends will find welcoming and helpful.

CHAPTER 1

The Ministry Marriage

". . . the two will become one flesh." This is a profound mystery— but I am talking about Christ and the church.
(Ephesians 5:31, 32)

"There is no more lovely, friendly, and charming relationship, communion or company than a good marriage."
— Martin Luther

When Deb and I met at Azusa Pacific University, I was a Kansas farm boy. She was a Southern California beach girl cheerleader. I was the lame freshman. She was the seasoned senior. We "fell" in love. (Yes, I will stop to acknowledge this as an act of God!) When we wed, I was 20 and Deb was 22. We both came from middle-class, working families with intact marriages. Our view of marriage was clouded by the stars in our eyes and, let's be honest, our hormones. We were the epitome of "naïve."

For all we did not know, we did understand that our marriage would be shaped by the pastoral ministry I was pursuing. Unlike most of our friends who were thinking about careers, paychecks, babies, and vacations, our hearts were thinking of how God was going to use us in full-time ministry. Our minds were filled with visions of seeing people come to know Christ, sharing platforms together to preach the gospel and discipling believers and growing churches. We knew ours would be a "ministry marriage."

Every marriage is sacred, commissioned to be involved in the specific ministries God calls a couple to do. Nevertheless, as you probably know if one or both of you is vocational ministry, there is something unique about a marriage shaped by daily ministry responsibilities. A "ministry marriage" comes with extraordinary challenges, responsibilities, opportunities, and blessings.

The Neglected Leadership Qualification

Deb and I have always been keenly aware of God's plain words about the role of elders or overseers. 1 Timothy 3:1-2 says, "Here is a trustworthy saying: Whoever aspires to be an overseer desires a noble task. Now the overseer is to be above reproach, faithful to his wife, temperate, self-controlled, respectable, hospitable, able to teach . . . ."

In this Scripture passage, God lays out three vital truths for our consideration:

- First, He says that He calls some believers to be overseers in the church and ministry—individuals who have already been involved in ministry. But there is an additional call to more fully engage as leaders and role models. If you're pastoring a church, planting a church, starting a ministry, taking over leadership of ministry, acting as an elder of a church, or in various other ways embracing Kingdom leadership, listen carefully to what God speaks specifically to you.
- Second, God identifies this leadership desire or involvement as a "noble" aspiration and pursuit. The New Testament is crystal clear that the two-tier system of sacred and secular or priest and commoner is no longer in play. Peter tells us unequivocally: "All believers are a kingdom of priests" (1 Peter 2:9). At the same time, though, Scripture tells us there are "overseers" who carry out a "noble task." This authority brings with it exceptional accountability (Heb. 13:17).

When Deb and I were dating, CB (citizen band) radios were the rage in my hometown of Ulysses, Kansas. Before cell phones, you could talk with other drivers through your CB radio. One of the main communication points was helping each other avoid speeding tickets from "Smokeys" (highway patrol). Every CB operator had a "handle"—a code name you used when you talked. My handle was, "Preacher Man." Deb was the one who confronted me with the double standard I was setting by calling myself "Preacher Man" and then breaking the law by asking for help to avoid any "Smokeys." Her message was clear: "Don't use the handle if you can't handle the accountability."

- Third, 1 Timothy 3 asserts that the overseer's character is actually what qualifies him or her for their service. The first phrase of the chapter, "above reproach," seems to be a summation of all the following descriptors. But note the first characteristic Paul underscores in 1 Timothy 3:2: "faithful to his wife." Push your pause button. When the phrase "faithful to his wife" is informed by the other scriptural directives concerning marriage, we understand that Paul is not just talking about staying married (no divorce) or even staying monogamous (no adultery). He's calling attention to the link between personal character, leadership integrity, and the condition of our marriages. The quality of the marriage is a leading indicator telling us that this leader is healthy enough to undertake a formal ministry role.

The Marriage Matters

Discussing the responsibilities of believers, Hebrews 13 emphasizes the practice of watching the lives of your leaders: "Remember your leaders, who spoke the word of God to you. Consider the outcome of their way of life and imitate their faith" (Heb. 13:2). If "faithful to his wife" is a key qualification for leadership, then the quality of the marriage is one of the primary aspects of a leader's "way of life." God's design for your marriage is that it be imitable.

One of my first negative memories of a pastor was Reverend Edwards.* I was in sixth grade and looked up to pastors like they were Supermen. Rev. Edwards was brilliant, funny, articulate, powerful and could pray like Daniel. He had a son about my age, and I ended up spending time in their home. It was there that Rev. Edwards lost his Superman cape. The way he treated his wife was frightening to me. He badgered her, belittled her, and ordered her around like she was his personal slave. I told my mom about it, and she encouraged me, "Just remember, Larry, pastors are human like the rest of us."

Mom's answer was accurate, helpful and also troublesome to me. I was beginning to understand that pastors were not the heroes from my comic books, but at the same time I thought, *If they are pastors, shouldn't their marriages be above average?* There was something not quite right. Rev. Edwards left our church after a couple of years, then he left ministry a few years later, then he left his wife. I was saddened but not surprised.

The Marriage Painting

Deb and I believe that God created the world and ordered human relationships to illustrate spiritual truths. He selected certain metaphors to display His plan and wisdom. Marriage is one of His best works. It's the symbol He chose to represent the relationship between Christ and His Church. God's plan is that the beauty of the "ministry marriage" would act as a magnet drawing others to Christ, to church, to ministry and to marriage itself. A Level 5 marriage is an ongoing painting of something so exquisite that it arrests the attention of the world and teaches something of the mystery between Christ and the Church. It is one of God's most glorious creations.

Before self-condemnation for your far-from-perfect marriage rushes in, let us be quick to point out that there are no more perfect marriages than there are perfect churches—zero, nada. Neither perfection will happen this side of Heaven. For now, we stumble along on feet crippled by sin. But in that flawed journey, we ask guiding questions: Are we moving in the right direction? Is the painting God intends taking shape? Is Level 5 in view? Is our union flourishing?

Perhaps one of our most common mistakes is failing to see our spouse as our brother or sister in Christ before we see him or her as our mate. We elevate our marriage identity above our spiritual identity. Deb and I have been struck by the revelation that we are only married for this life but will be united in the family of Christ forever. This means our spiritual family relationship trumps our marriage relationship: He's my brother, then my husband. She's my sister, then my wife.

Marriages are microcosms of the church. In our marriages, we learn to pray, to listen, to serve, to practice our spiritual gifts, to confess and forgive, to nurture and teach, to bear long, to show grace, to disciple one another, to express our burdens, to worship and sing, to share the table, to express our thanksgiving, and to demonstrate the fruit of his Spirit. Ministry begins in our own marriage with our brother or sister. The salient question is, "Are we doing 'church' well in our homes so that we can do 'church' well in the church?"

If you have children, this question is meant to be applied to your family. What a powerful testimony to the world when a ministry family unites under the banner of Christ to move forward together on mission with Jesus. However, as our children age, we are less and less in control of this "togetherness". When the world sees "PK's" [Pastor's Kids] crash and burn, tongues will wag and their skeptical comments pierce our hearts. Losing a child to a wayward lifestyle can easily, but unnecessarily, sideline a pastoral couple, temporarily or permanently.

Early in our pastoral careers, one of our staff pastors came to us ashamed to share that his eldest teen daughter had become pregnant. Fortunately, the beautiful outcome after this family disclosed the news to our small church, was the embrace, love and acceptance they felt from the church family. In spite of Sheila's mistake, this family experienced the church's love and were assured they would be cared for well during the pregnancy and afterwards, as well. You could almost hear their sigh of relief when others came alongside of them. Their ministry continued to flourish, and the family recovered from this unexpected situation. This is the body of Christ coming alongside ministry families to share their burdens, weeping together when there is weeping.

The Balls You Can Drop—And the Ones You Can't

Deb has been the primary voice calling our ministry staff at Light & Life toward the priority of their marriage. Although I share her thinking, she has a unique passion and gifting in this regard. One of her mantras, which she impresses on our staff is, "Marriage before ministry! If you mix up the order, you mess up the ministry!" Make no mistake. Successful ministries aren't indicators that all is well in the home. The smile up front on Sunday morning does not necessarily show you what's behind the doors during the week.

If we think of marriage and ministry life as balls we're juggling, you might get a really clear picture of the difference between the two. Drop a rubber ball, and it will bounce back. Drop a crystal ball, and it will shatter. In life, it's all about knowing which balls you can drop and which ones you can't. Marriage is one of your crystal balls; ministry is a rubber ball. Better to drop a ministry than shatter a marriage. *Pay special attention to the crystal balls in your life.*

Our children are also crystal balls. Although we're not really addressing parenting in this book, the children of ministry marriages will be significantly impacted and benefit or suffer from our marriage relationship. They will affect the seasons in our marriage like none other. Deb and I have one biological daughter, Lindsey, and one daughter, Anjelica, whom we adopted as an older teen from a tough situation. Additionally, we have had a dozen "kids" who have lived with us, some for as long as two years. How we have handled our marriage has influenced our children. Remember the best thing you can do for your kids is flourish as a couple and grow a Level 5 marriage.

CHAPTER 2

Five Levels of Marriage: Which One Are You?

*"... I have come that they may have
life, and have it to the full."*
(John 10:10)

*"Love at first sight is easy to understand; it's when
two people have been looking at each other
for a lifetime that it becomes a miracle."*
—Sam Levenson, film actor, director

On April 29, 2011, the Archbishop of Canterbury stood before Prince William and Catherine Middleton in the most widely viewed wedding in history. Archbishop Rowan Williams slowly intonated sage words, calling the couple to a holy vision for their future together. He partially described what we're calling a "Level 5" marriage. Here are a few sentences of his address:

... Marriage is intended to be a way in which man and woman help each other to become what God meant each one to be, their deepest and truest selves. ... In a sense, every wedding is a royal wedding with the bride and the groom as king and queen of creation, making a new life together so that life can flow through them into the future.[1]

Your wedding was also royal. Whether it happened in a Las Vegas chapel or a formal church sanctuary, or with beach sand between your toes or in Westminster Abbey, your nuptials were miraculous. It is irrelevant if ten people or 162 million (viewers reported for Prince William and Catherine's wedding) heard your vows. Your Father, King of the Universe, was listening and working.

Assessing Your Marriage

When you spoke your vows, God performed a supernatural marvel, birthing a new entity—your marriage. Like a baby that requires nurturing, attention, love and discipline, your marriage also needs these essential elements to help it grow up and flourish. Without them, your marriage could become stuck in the infant, toddler, or teen stage and never mature. Few of us would argue that most of the marriages today are simply surviving; very few actually thrive. Marriages may be growing older, but unfortunately, they're not growing better.

But God has a different plan.

As Archbishop Williams implied, God is looking for disciples and marriages to light the world on fire with His truth and love through their unique personalities. He desires for His people, who are committed to helping each other, to have the beautiful and impactful marriage He designed it to be—one of intimacy and impact. The objective of this caliber of marriage is captured in the archbishop's powerful words: "a new life together so that life can flow through them into the future."[2]

As I mentioned before, Deb and I have carefully observed hundreds of marriages in our various contexts. Together, we have grieved over dried-up marriages and have cheered for those marriages that are overflowing with life. More importantly, we have studied our own marriage that has gone through seasons of shallowness and abundance. As we explained in the Introduction of this book, we are taking a cue from Exponential's five levels of church multiplication framework and describing the levels of marriage intimacy and impact as Levels 1 through 5.

Classifications can be misleading and counterproductive. This happens when we assign too much weight or rigidity to the labels. On the other hand, a five-level scale can prove immensely valuable when we use it appropriately. It can help answer important questions like:

- Where's our marriage now? (your marriage reality)
- Where has our marriage been? (your marriage story)
- Where do we want our marriage to go? (your marriage vision)
- What are key indicators of health and vitality? (your marriage values)

We hope you're reading this book together as a couple. If so, we urge you to read through this chapter but refrain from discussing the level you each think your marriage is. Once you have both read the chapter, we encourage each of you to write down your personal assessment of your marriage (putting it on paper/screen keeps you true to your first opinion). Then find an uninterrupted space and share your perspectives with each other.

We also encourage you to understand each of the levels, not only to improve your own marriage but also for the sake of helping other marriages. This tool can become an important aid to helping you assist and teach other couples to honestly assess their marriage, move forward, and flourish.

Five Levels of Marriage

Regardless of any life circumstances that may have affected your lives and marriage, the two of you are responsible for the kind of marriage you build. God has provided you with all of the resources you need. Imagine you and your spouse building a home, and Home Depot delivers everything it will take to build an incredible mansion. You don't have to manufacture a thing. It's all there: the cement for the foundation, the support beams, the windows, the doors, the cabinets, even the toilets and toilet roll holders. In addition, the blueprints and building instructions are all loaded on a provided laptop. Just like building a home, your mission is to take what God supplies and build something to live in and share with family and friends. A place of refuge, rest, nurture, training and joy.

Some couples take their hammers and quickly grab a few of the resources to nail together a one-bedroom shack, which will eventually include a separation wall in the middle of the shack to avoid one another. Others put in a little more effort to construct a small but comfortable 1,200-square-foot two-bedroom rambler. It houses one room with twin beds for mom and dad and one room for the kids. The three TV sets and microwave allow the family to live together without getting too personal.

Still, other couples use more of the building supplies. They decide to take time and invest some real sweat to design and build a 2,000-square-foot, two-story three-bedroom home. The house has a nice family room where the family shares laughter in front of the TV, plays cards and has some family devotions.

A few couples use even more of the building provisions and continue constructing, remodeling and expanding until they have a beautiful four-bedroom home. One room is a large master bedroom, a room of retreat and intimacy for husband and wife. Two rooms are for the kids to grow in with one room for guests enjoying the wisdom and hospitality of the home.

Only a handful of marrieds use *all* of the materials God has supplied. Over the years, they learn new skills so they can continually upgrade and enlarge their home. Ultimately, they end up living in an exquisite five-bedroom mansion with all the rooms of the four-bedroom home plus even a large chapel.

Here's the great news: God has personally invited and equipped you to build the mansion. You will have the earthly privilege of living in what you build for the rest of your life. Plus, you'll be eternally rewarded for the ministry you provided to other ministry couples. The work is worth it.

First, you need to discern where you are in your marriage. Much like a GPS that relies on location to calculate the route for your destination, until you know and acknowledge where you are in your marriage, you'll never get to where you want to be.

Level 1: The Consumer Marriage

The Level 1 marriage is in decline, existing in survival mode and slowly losing any intimacy and impact it has had. We define it as marriage where the spouses do a lot of "taking" but little "giving."

People marry for various reasons, but almost all of us wed because we believe life will be better together than separate. Consumers want to receive "goods or services" from their decisions. Granted, there is some consumer in each of us. The destructive poison of consumption kills when it becomes the predominant posture of either or both spouses.

I think of Nabal and Abigail's marriage we find in the Old Testament. Nabal epitomizes the consumeristic nature of a Level 1 husband. 1 Samuel 25 tells the story of what happened when David showed up at Nabal's farm in need. After spending the last year protecting Nabal, David rightly expects Nabal to help him. But the plot twists when Nabal refuses to assist David. When Abigail hears of her husband's selfishness, she sees her husband's arrogance for the foolishness it is. Without consulting with her husband, Abigail acts to right this travesty and begs David for mercy. Their marriage is void of any trust, communication and wisdom. Not surprisingly, the marriage ends shortly after—a lot of taking with no giving.

Level 1 Marriage Characteristics

A marriage in decline will have specific characteristics and warning signs:

Too many withdrawals with no deposits. Several telling statements describe the attitude of the people in a Level 1 marriage:

You exist for me.
It's my way or no way.
What's in it for me?
Marriage is for making me happy.
You owe me sex tonight.
Give me more "me" time.
This isn't working for me.

The consumer marriage becomes a bank where one or both partners make emotional withdrawals without concerning themselves with deposits. Emotional deposits happen when you speak or act in your spouse's love language. Small withdrawals occur through daily routines of living; large deductions happen when we demonstrate selfishness in the form of neglect, insensitivity, conflict, or ignorance. Soon, the emotional account is overdrawn, and marriage bankruptcy is near.

Too often, we've seen the destructive consequences that happen when spouses try and run a marriage on consumer credit—the lie that I can "buy now, pay later." I can "charge" the emotions or actions I need from my spouse and "make it up to them" later. This approach can work somewhat in the short term if you're paying off your balance at least monthly. But a minority of Americans pay off their credit card balances monthly; even fewer pay off on their emotional marriage "debts."

When it comes to the family, it is easy to see how some ministry families crash and burn over time when the emotional debt gets too high. The kids grow up feeling neglected due to the lack of positive relational deposits made into their emotional bank accounts. When a correction needs to be made, the deficit is so large that the child flips out, leaving a wake of devastation in the family. We have so often seen this pattern that we identify it as, "The rules without relationship = rebellion" problem. These types of experiences will erode the testimony and mission of the family as it seeks to serve as the body of Christ.

A toxic environment. A Level 1 marriage is a toxic environment. The wife feels misunderstood, unloved, and either unappreciated or underappreciated. The husband feels disrespected and disillusioned. He doesn't know a love language exists. She doesn't even want to speak his.

Emotional and physical distance. In a Level 1 marriage, interpersonal communication is impersonal, distant or accusatory. Sex is either non-existent or practiced on a solely physical level of using the spouse to fulfill personal desires.

There is often a cavernous private/public gap. Behind closed doors, the marriage is distant or isolated, non-communicative, conflictual or badgering. In public, however, a Christian veneer of smiley-faced politeness or even syrupy spiritual sweetness covers the crevices in the relationship.

Ministry is an escape. The ministry of a Level 1 marriage doesn't escape toxicity. Ministry is usually an escape from the marriage. Long hours away are excused under the guise of "doing the Lord's work." Teamwork is non-existent. Often, only one spouse is active in church while the other distances himself or herself physically or emotionally from church ministry. If the couple has children, this same dysfunctional dynamic would be clearly seen. The pain of the marriage usually manifests through the actions of the children. This marriage and family are far from being together as one unit.

When we think of a marriage that used ministry as an escape, our first thoughts go to Curtis and Laney. After seven years of marriage, this couple could no longer hide the cracks in their private lives behind the professional smiles of ministry. Curtis was angry because his ministry wasn't growing, and his sex life was far less then he desired. He felt he deserved the porn he started to secretly use to entertain himself.

Laney was into her job and ignoring Curtis. She had tried to be the pastor's wife Curtis expected, but when he seemed more consumed with ministry success than the needs of people, she became unmotivated. Laney found more and more distractions to help her escape. Between her college girlfriends, her job, and her romance novels, she could get what she wanted—with or without Curtis.

Their Level 1 marriage was dragging along, headed for divorce. Praise God! They sent up a Hail Mary and reached out for help. As they began accessing the resources available to them and counteracting the Level 1 characteristics that had taken over their marriage, their relationship began to grow again. Like we said before (we want to make sure you get this), you *can* move from your current marriage level.

Level 2: The Convenient Marriage

The Level 2 marriage is a plateaued relationship built around what must get done to "get by the best we can." It exists as a convenience in life. The relationship is usually held in place by one or more of the following: the ministry, the kids, the bills, his job, people's opinions, the church, friends, the house, the cost of living—or some other reality that makes it more convenient to stay together than to separate.

Sometimes we call this the "twenty-five-year marriage." After twenty-five years of changing diapers, doing science projects, driving to soccer, and taking prom pictures, one spouse (usually the wife) rolls over in bed, looks at the only person left in the house and says two things: "Who are you, really?" and "Since the kids have left, I can too." Plateaus can last a lifetime but often end at a cliff.

Jim and Liz had been in their ministry marriage for twelve years. People inside the church and at their kid's elementary school thought well of their marriage. Liz was the sweetest person you could hope to meet. The first to volunteer or go out of her way to do something kind for someone. Jim was steady, sturdy, and smart. He was the soccer coach for all their kids' teams. They weren't Ken and Barbie, but they were a seemingly solid couple. Until, to the shock of all, Jim left Liz for the younger third-grade Christian school teacher.

"What happened?" I asked Jim.

His reply is instructive for every marriage: "After the first year, it was never about 'us' anymore. It was about her, or me, or the kids, or the church. We lost the 'us.' I couldn't see myself living the rest of my life without an 'us,' so when someone came along that made it all about 'us,' I went for it."

Level 2 marriages usually revolve around an often undetected or unconfessed question and rationale: "Is life better for *me*, with or without my current spouse? If my life is better with her/him, then I stay because it's better for me." Or sometimes the question will be, "Is life better for the *kids* if I stay or if I divorce? If it's better for the kids to stay married, then I do—at least for now."

Level 2 Marriage Characteristics

Conversations of convenience. Level 2 marriages use communication as a utilitarian tool to get the job done. "Who's taking which kid where? When is this bill due? Deacon Jones wants us to come to dinner on Friday. Don't forget you have nursery duty this Sunday. My folks are coming next week. Can you help me paint the baby's room?"

Conversations are convenient but don't touch on communion. Deep talks about personal feelings, spiritual passions, fears, and dreams are either absent or rarities. Neither spouse really knows where the other one is in their heart. This same dynamic plays out in their parenting. Since they have not been able to attain a depth of intimacy in their marriage, they struggle to know how to relate to their children's emotions. Interactions commonly focus on tasks needing to be accomplished, assignments at school, what is coming up on the calendar for the family, and so on. This type of interaction becomes stale once the child reaches adolescence. Sadly, by that time the child chooses to go elsewhere to find the intimacy she or he craves.

Sparse spiritual interaction. In a Level 2 marriage, any spiritual interactions happen individually and rarely as a couple. Perhaps both spouses are disciplined about having a "quiet time," but they share nothing from those times with each other. Prayer together as a couple happens mostly before a meal or at devotions with the kids. Scripture reading is a solo event, not a joint experience. Spiritual conversations are substituted with ministry conversations to "get 'er done."

Lack of intimacy. Busyness that crowds out intimacy is often a hallmark of Level 2 marriages. Aspirations of educational, vocational, parental, church growth or ministry success keep the marriage focused on the "to do list" instead of on the "us" list. There is a lack of effort to understand the emotions, desires, goals, priorities, passions, or values of your spouse. You go just deep enough to keep the marriage machine running.

Ministry is ineffective or barren. In Scripture, we can look at the union of King David and Michal (daughter of King Saul) as an example of Level 2 marriage where ministry suffers. Setting aside the vastly different polygamous culture, we see a couple who failed to understand one another. At the start, we know that Michal was in love with David, the hero of Israel (1 Samuel 18:20). Later, when Saul sends men to kill David, Michal lies to protect David and then lies to protect herself. It was convenient. The couple is together, helping one another to help themselves.

Yet for all this devotion, we see no depth to their relationship. While we only have fragments of information, David and Michal weren't emotionally and spiritually in sync. David was passionate about worship of the true God of Judah. Michal was primarily concerned about her husband's political and public image, probably because his public persona affected her own. She misunderstood her husband and worked from a different script, an alternative set of values. Consequently, when David laid aside his kingly garments to dance uncovered in worship before the ark of God, Michal was incensed. David let her know she was on the wrong page, basically saying, "There's a lot more where that came from." The result of their convenient but shallow marriage was not divorce, but barrenness. It failed to produce offspring.

In a Level 2 Marriage, ministry happens but is mostly ineffective or barren. Ministry is done more individually than collaboratively, and ministry behaviors become ruts that keep the machine running. Level 2 marriages reflect few conversations about ministry passions or dreams. Ministry is done at the same place but not truly together. The couple maintains the ministry image, but the fire is gone. The same lack-luster lifestyle is seen in the family interactions. It is not uncommon to hear grunts and groans when church is mentioned. Church life is now death to the family, just one more thing "to do" rather than collaborate on together.

People were shocked when Samantha left Ben after twenty-two years. Deb and I were not. We knew Ben was having an affair—with ministry. For years, Ben had been cheating his marriage to woo his church's affection. Samantha had been a necessary support to keep his ministry fling active. She felt it. Ben would never admit it. Finally, Samantha (wrongly) decided to have her own affair with a man who could care less about ministry. Everyone sided with Ben.

Marriages aren't static. You can never really put a marriage in neutral. Each day, they are either building or losing intimacy. Satan, society, and our sinfulness create a perpetual downward pull on our marriages. It's like thinking you can put your car in neutral while sitting on a hill. The gearshift may technically say you're in neutral, but soon you're rolling downhill. Convenient marriages are losing ground even when one or both spouses think the marriage is okay because it's in neutral.

Paul didn't write Galatians 6:9 specifically about marriage, but I think it's a general principle we can apply to our marriages: "Let us not become weary in doing good, for at the proper time we will reap a harvest if we do not give up." Marriages need consistent focus and pursuit to do good for one another.

Level 3: The Committed Marriage

A Level 3 ministry marriage is the "good" marriage—a solid, devoted relationship. This marriage profile is marked by kind and authentic, albeit underdeveloped, "togetherness." In a Level 3 ministry marriage, the wedding vows are not superficial, temporary words spoken to launch the honeymoon. The promises are genuine and personal. This is the "committed marriage," which gives rise to a mostly satisfying life as a couple and family.

This is the marriage TV shows depicted when Deb and I were growing up: Ozzie and Harriet, Lucy and Ricky, Mike and Carol Brady. There were adventures, problems, mistakes, family challenges, and friendship trials, but the "D-word "of divorce never surfaced. There was commitment, kept promises, care, compassion and moments of "cheek pecking." The spouses knew their roles. They stayed in their lanes, and everything worked out just fine within thirty minutes or so.

The Level 3 marriage has moved beyond much of the self-centeredness of Levels 1 and 2 to a dedication to the well-being of the marriage. There is a determination to fulfill the roles of being a good husband or wife—an overall desire to bless your spouse. At Level 3, Deb and I have heard statements like:

We just want our marriage to please God.
Our family must be a testimony to the church.
We are focused on being role models to other marriages.
My husband is nearly perfect.
My wife is the godliest and hottest woman in our church.
The family that prays together, stays together.

Most of these can be good statements unless they're covering up a different reality or inhibiting a deeper level of intimacy and authenticity. A Level 3 marriage often has an invisible veneer of pride that covers the beauty of these relationships. The marriage depends on self-discipline instead of the Spirit of God.

Level 3 marriages need to be valued for what they are but also seen for what they are not. They fail to live in the rich intimacy and multiplicative impact God intends for marriage. We suggest couples ask what can be hard but nevertheless important questions: "Have we settled for good enough? Is this the marriage God dreams for us? How do we take our marriage from good to great? Are we flourishing?"

The first eleven years of our ministry marriage were what we would consider a "Level 3" marriage. We weren't really flourishing. I was the minister, and Deb was my helper. She fulfilled whatever wife or ministry role I thought was necessary. We were deeply committed to each other, to our senior pastor, and to our church's ministry. We had the ideal marriage and could tell other couples how to be just like us.

For every problem, we had a Bible verse in hand. Any ongoing difficulty was simply a matter of disobedience or unbelief. In hindsight, I realize that while I listened to Deb, I filtered her responses through my own desires and needs. Our ministry was solid and succeeding; all seemed good.

We didn't realize, however, the unrealized relational richness available to us. We failed to understand how shallow the roots of our marriage really were. Our "oneness" didn't stem from a fully transparent embrace of the individuality of one another but from a gritted-teeth determination to be obedient to God and appear unified.

Level 3 Marriage Characteristics

A lack of vulnerability. At Level 3, communication is not sporadic (Level 1) or focused on the functional (Level 2) but now consists of more personal dynamics. Sharing about the journey of life is more frequent. There are occasional conversations about "us" or about "our marriage." However, we still see a lack of deep vulnerability at this level. Spouses either do not understand their own hearts, are ignorant of how to share deeply, or just don't feel the safety they need to talk candidly and deeply. As a result, answers are shaped toward what's *expected* in the role or what will "bless" the ministry or what will be the "Christian" thing to say.

Service out of duty. Level 3 marriages clearly have signs of serving one another. However, this service springs more from duty than delight. There is an ineptness at seeing things from your spouse's viewpoint and a reluctance to apologize deeply. Couples filter their actions through the mindset of, "How will the church see this?" or "Is this what the perfect ministry spouse would do, say, buy or enjoy?"

Inward-focused ministry. Significant ministry results can accrue from a Level 3 marriage, and the good life can be lived at this level. What we see at this level, however, centers on motive. In the "committed marriage," ministry dynamics focus on working together as a team for the success of the ministry. There is a passion for ministering together, but the focus is inward—building *our* church or ministry more than God's Kingdom. The question is, "What role needs to be filled so our church/ministry will grow?" rather than, "What are my passions/gifts/calling, and how can I blend those into God's vision for our church?"

Level 3 marriages tend toward helping each other succeed for the sake of your reputation as much as for the cause of the mission. There is sincerity about glorifying God and building His work, but that sincerity is diffused by the pride of increasing status of self, marriage and ministry. This can cause significant impact on the children of these couples. The unrealistic expectation that our kids will "do the work of ministry" because they are "pastor's" kids, puts undue pressure on them. The family works together, but at whose expense? If the ministry "pride" of Level 3 families drives the actions, eventually breakdown will occur.

Warning!

The Level 3 marriage is vulnerable to sudden breakdowns. Sometimes, one of the spouses just gets tired of playing the role, or of being the helper, or of building the machine, or of keeping the ministry factory running, or of just being mom, or of not having their personal dreams valued and championed. The list goes on. Suddenly, to the shock of the church and the clueless spouse, he or she runs off with someone who really "gets them."

Suzy and Ted were becoming well known in ministry. Her book was a national best seller, and she was frequently flying places to speak. Ted was an effective preacher, and his church was growing. Their kids were role models in Sunday school. They vacationed in Hawaii in the winter and the Rockies in the summer. They led marriage retreats to teach the biblical rules for effective marriages. So when Ted suddenly ran off with his secretary, both Suzy and the church were stunned. Their best friends, Tom and Peggy, however, weren't surprised. They had seen Suzy and Ted tiring in their efforts to maintain an example of a marriage based more on willpower than transparency and Spirit dependency.

This is not the story of most Level 3 "committed marriages." Most go the distance. But the journey is a march instead of a dance. True freedom is only found in Level 4 and 5 marriages.

Level 4: The Collaborative Marriage

The Level 4 marriage has moved into most of God's idea of "oneness." The couple is flourishing both married and as individuals. We think the word "collaborative" is a strong descriptor. Technically, the word means "two or more people working together to achieve a special purpose." Some definitions add the concept of "equality." So the idea becomes, "two equals working together to do something that cannot be accomplished alone."

Deb and I recently decided to take a cruise, which led to the time-consuming task of shopping for a cruise. We looked at cruise line after cruise line. Each of their offerings were arranged into three categories: good, better, best. We wanted the "best" but didn't know whether we could afford it. There was a significant cost to moving from good to better to best. (We chose "better.")

The same is true in moving from a "good" marriage at Level 3 to a "better" marriage at Level 4. Level 4 costs something. That's why most marriages live at Level 3 or below. Spouses either don't know how to attain Level 4 or aren't willing to pay the price to get there.

The first couple on earth, Adam and Eve, offers us a prime example of "collaboration." I've heard sermons and teaching that wrongly interpret Genesis and assume that Scripture implies Adam needed an "assistant," so God gave him a helper. However, the Hebrew translation of the word "helper" in this passage is *ezer*, which means "to rescue, save." The transliteration shows us that God Himself is helping Adam by delivering him from his aloneness—not giving him a cook and cleaner. In Eve, God creates a helper of equal gifting and value so that together, Adam and Eve can collaborate to achieve a special purpose: procreation and reproduction.

This miracle of reproduction is a clear illustration of "synergy." In dictionary terms, synergy is "the product of what happens when the interaction of two or more agents produces a combined effect greater than the sum of their separate effects." So 1 + 1 does not equal 2. Instead, 1 + 1 = 3, as in Adam + Eve = Cain. Out of Adam and Eve's intimacy came an impact upon the world. Level 4 marriages boast a synergy that's able to yield something that can only be produced working together.

Of course, many marriages either choose not to have or cannot have offspring. So we want to be clear in saying that God's intended collaborative purpose for marriage is not limited to, nor even focused on, physical children. Instead God's greater purpose is for husband and wife to work together to bring forth *spiritual* children—individuals who have been born again by the power of the gospel. This is disciple-making at its core. Starting with our children, the Level 4 marriage is concerned that first, their children are discipled into the ways of Christ so they too can become multiplicative, Kingdom-focused as they grow up. When this happens, the family is excited to collaborate together for the sake of Christ's mission of love.

The collaborative marriage has moved into the power of oneness for the sake of the gospel. The intimacy of the marriage is producing impact in ministry. No longer is one mate only helping the other succeed in his or her ministry role (Level 3). Together, they're now working in their strengths toward a common goal. This mindset overflows to the children as well.

This collaborative flow of togetherness is what Paul was referring to in 1 Corinthians 12:4, "Now to each one the manifestation of the Spirit is given for the common good," and further on, "But in fact God has placed the parts in the body, every one of them, just as he wanted them to be. If they were all one part, where would the body be? As it is, there are many parts, but one body." The synergy of "oneness" is demonstrated in this marriage and family. Each lead in areas where they're gifted. Their hearts beat together. They're flourishing.

Characteristics of a Level 4 Marriage

Kingdom multiplication over ministry. In a Level 4 marriage, the priority is the Kingdom being extended over the ministry "succeeding." This Kingdom focus liberates both spouses to work freely in the area of their individual passions, callings and giftings, yet maintain a unity of vision and effort. They yearn to "make disciples" in every way possible. New disciples, leaders, ministries, and churches are the reproductive result of their marriage.

Few people stop to consider the apostle Peter's marriage. From what little we know about it in Scripture, we might guess it was a Level 4 marriage. Luke 4:38 tells us that Simon had a house, he was married and that his mother-in-law, who lived with them, was ill. We also know that Simon and his wife asked Jesus to heal this mother-in-law. Jesus touches her hand, and Luke's Gospel tells us that Peter's mother-in-law rose up and began preparing dinner for Jesus and His crew.

The next place we see Peter's wife mentioned is in 1 Corinthians 9:5 where Paul asks, "Don't we have the right to take a believing wife along with us, as do the other apostles and the Lord's brothers and Cephas (Peter)?" From this scripture, we know that Peter's wife was a believer and a fellow minister who traveled with Peter in their ministry endeavors. These scriptures show us that Peter cared about what his wife cared about. Together, they had faith in the power of Jesus to transform bodies and lives. Together, they were willing to leave their home behind to pursue the mission God had called them to. Together, they traveled facing hardships and persecutions. They were co-laborers in the harvest. Yes, Peter gets all the notoriety, but we may be surprised when we learn what impact this marriage had on the ministry.

The husband sees his wife as an equal. Multiplying ministry flows from high degrees of honor and vulnerability. If a husband holds a mental or emotional position of superiority to his wife based on his maleness, the couple can never move to this marriage level. When Deb or I see someone who considers himself the "greater" laying down his life for the "weaker" vessel, we also find an unrealized potential in both intimacy and impact. Something is askew in the relationship, inhibiting full vulnerability and hindering even the husband's most sincere attempts to honor his wife.

The Level 4 marriage is marked by an unselfish desire in both spouses to help each other become whom God created them to be as both a person and minister. The marriage is not an entity that must look good for the church or ministry . . . it's just an authentically robust relationship, confident about letting the church search behind the closed doors of their home. When it comes to the family, there is an authentic honesty to how the family is doing. There is a keen realization that they truly are "Better Together" when it comes to working in the church because each one knows they are an important part of the big picture.

When Lindsey, our biological daughter, was eleven years old, God called our church to become a center for church planting. Having never personally planted a church we felt God might be calling us to start the first one ourselves on a Sunday evening. We needed to figure out how to plant a church ourselves if this new vision was to be a permanent reality for our church's future. As a family, we talked about the impact planting an evening service would have on our family. We talked about how Mondays might feel hard when the alarm clock went off because of the late night cleanup that came after service. When it came down to making our final decision whether we would plant the first church, Lindsey enthusiastically said, "Yes! Let's do this!" She was "all in" for this new family adventure with God.

Serving each other out of love. Level 4 spouses find delight in serving one another. In the collaborative marriage overflowing with humility and love, acts of service are treated as a privilege, not a chore. Before I was married, I watched my sister and brother-in-law's marriage and was profoundly influenced by the joy they had.

"What's the secret of your marriage," I asked them one day.

"When you are in love with a person, their need or desire becomes your opportunity to bless both of your hearts," my sister explained.

As I mentioned above, moving from a Level 3 to Level 4 marriage comes with a price. The toll is a deeper dying to self without denying the "self" God made you to be. You limit your own freedoms to pursue your dreams to help your spouse realize their dreams. The same attitude flows through the Level 4 couple's parenting. The children feel supported and loved as they seek God about their dreams and callings.

Deepening spiritual maturity. Level 4 marriages have an intensity of spiritual engagement that is both personal and communal. Each spouse has an intimate spiritual relationship with Jesus independent of their husband/wife. Each of their lives is rich and flourishing in the spiritual disciplines. And they regularly share their individual spiritual lives with each other.

There is an "iron sharpening iron" dimension to their spiritual lives. Each spouse "gives and receives" in prayer, biblical understanding, exhortations and spiritual discussions. There is a "collaboration" in the process of spiritual maturation. Spouses operate as sister and brother in Christ, instead of the sex-motivated lovers that Hollywood unrealistically expects them to be.

In a Level 4 family, the kids have been discipled well, which helps them freely share their faith with others. When someone needs prayer, it is not an afterthought for the Level 4 family. Together they seek God for the needs of others.

Side note—We know that once children reach adulthood they are responsible for their lives. At times they might choose more destructive paths through life choices, or traumatic things might happen to them, impacting their ability to make wise decisions. Too often we have seen ministry couples doubt their good parenting or their own spiritual vitality. They may end up blaming themselves for the change in their child's life. We want to say that you cannot blame yourselves for your child's adult decisions. Life happens, so stay on your knees and pray, rather than beating yourselves up for their mistakes.

In 2006, I received my Doctorate in Ministry. In 2014, Deb received the same degree from a different seminary. But something changed in our ministry during those eight years. We went from being a "church-growth" church to a "missional" and "church-planting" church. One of the main reasons for this transformation was the personal change in our hearts and marriage. We became captivated by the concept of "the Kingdom of God" and the "big C church." We challenged each other to reread the Gospels to see what Jesus really valued. Deb exhorted me and pointed out areas where my pride and status seeking were still over-influencing our ministry. We fasted and prayed. Our unity in marriage and ministry advanced dramatically. Our co-laboring has yielded more "spiritual offspring" than in all of our previous years of marriage.

Level 5: The Communion Marriage

We all know the perfect marriage doesn't exist. That idea should be off the table. However, God desires Level 5 marriages for all of us. Let that sink in. *God wants a marriage for you that is overflowing with both intimacy and impact.* We believe these marriages are possible through the truth of God's Word and the power of His Spirit. In fact, our purpose in writing this book is to spark a quest in you for a flourishing marriage.

We quite purposefully titled this Level 5 marriage the "communion marriage." To grasp this dream God has for our marriages, we must understand the biblical and theological foundation of a Level 5 marriage. These authoritative truths deliver us from cultural lies and empower us to write a different story in and through our marriages. We find these biblical principles primarily in the original marriage of Adam and Eve and in the communion of Christ and His bride. Communion is life-giving!

The only flawless Level 5 marriage existed for a short time in the Garden of Eden between Adam and Eve. We see it described in a few select verses in Genesis. As we study their marriage, words like "united, oneness, intimacy, vulnerability, security, liberty, fearlessness, knowingness, mutuality, sharing, productivity, multiplicative and communion" come to mind.

Genesis 2:24 explains the separation of an individual from their parents and the unification with their spouse: "That is why a man leaves his father and mother and is united to his wife, and they become one flesh." In this scripture, the Hebrew translation of "united" is *dabaq*, and it can literally mean "to be glued together." Two formerly independent entities join to form a new entity of one. Adam and Eve certainly retained their individuality as we see in Genesis 3. Yet there was a new reality about them that would impact their relationship and productivity for the remainder of their lives.

CHAPTER 2 | FIVE LEVELS OF MARRIAGE: WHICH ONE ARE YOU?

Genesis 2:25 describes the depth and security of this new relationship: "Adam and his wife were both naked, and they felt no shame." This nakedness was not merely physical. The physical nakedness was primarily an outward illustration of an inward reality. In the love of God and each other was security, allowing for personal, emotional, and spiritual vulnerability. This vulnerability freed them from any concern over covering any part of themselves—no shame, insecurity, low self-esteem or comparison. They were part of one another and wanted only the best for their spouse.

The depth of security generated a pervasive liberty. When I read Genesis 2:25, it makes me think of the wildly popular quote, *"Sing like no one is listening. Love like you've never been hurt.*

Dance like nobody's watching, and live like it's Heaven on earth" (attributed to Susanna Clark and Richard Leigh). [3] For us, they are provocative lines of wishful thinking and dreaming. For Adam and Eve, they lived it.

Adam and Eve experienced a life-giving spiritual communion with one another and with God. In Genesis 1:28, we discover God's provision for them: "God blessed them and said to them, 'Be fruitful and multiply . . . '" His blessing was this "oneness" to overcome their "aloneness." The blessing included the power to use their "oneness," according to His design, and multiply. Their oneness could result in others being created. Knowing He had given them this ability, God simultaneously gives them the mission and command: "Be fruitful and multiply." Their marriage would result in multiplication for God's Kingdom.

God carries out this "communion," (both physically and spiritually) motif even after the fall. Genesis 4:1 says, "Adam made love to his wife Eve, and she became pregnant and gave birth to Cain. She said, 'With the help of the LORD I have brought forth a man.'" The

King James Version more fully captures the meaning of the Hebrew word *yada*: "Adam *knew* his wife, Eve, and she conceived . . ." They "knew" each other not just physically but also spiritually. They had intimate communion, and the result was both spiritual and physical offspring. Not only a son, named Cain, but by the end of Genesis 4, eight generations of children had been produced with thousands of individuals. They had fulfilled God's command, physically and spiritually "multiplying."

On this biblical footing, we aspire to Level 5 marriage. Adam and Eve's account foreshadows the intimacy of marriage and the resulting potential of multiplicative impact. Our "communion" with Christ and our marriage partner is life-giving both to us and through us to others. As we "know" Christ and "know" our spouse, more "spiritual" children can be born.

Level 5 Marriage in the Bible

Aquila and Priscilla are the best New Testament example of what was likely a Level 5 marriage. Their love for the Lord, for each other, and for those without Christ (or naïve in Christ, like Apollos) gave birth to many spiritual children. They lived in communion with Christ and with one another. From that place, they poured out God's love to others.

The term "communion" derives from the Latin word *communio* (meaning "sharing in common"), which translates to the Greek word *koinōnía* in 1 Corinthians 10:16: "The cup of blessing which we bless, is it not the communion of the blood of Christ? The bread which we break, is it not the communion of the body of Christ?"

The first communion instituted a symbolic act which, when taken in faith, would release to us the grace necessary to establish, maintain, and renew our oneness with Christ and one another. It unleashes

CHAPTER 2 | FIVE LEVELS OF MARRIAGE: WHICH ONE ARE YOU?

the power of the cross for our sins that separate us from one another. This communion compels us to cover one another's sins with grace. It inspires us to give ourselves to bless our spouse.

In the communion marriage, we seek a deeper fellowship with the Spirit of Christ and the spirit of our spouse. We look to the power of the sacrifice of Christ (which gives rise to communion) as a model for how to pursue this intimacy. 1 John 3:16 defines the truest manifestation of love: "This is how we know what love is: Jesus Christ laid down his life for us. And we ought to lay down our lives for our brothers and sisters."

Through the cross, we know we are loved. Our wife is our closest sister; our husband is our nearest brother. Through our acts of sacrifice, our spouses discover they are loved. In this mutual giving, communion grows. In a Level 5 marriage, self is not denied or minimized, but self-interest is surrendered to serve your spouse.

It is the self-giving—this earnest communion of life; this moment-by-moment responsiveness to the Spirit; and daily surrender to the best interests of your wife/husband—that most clearly defines God's idea for your marriage. While the foundation and power of this type of marriage are biblical, theological, and spiritual, we see the incarnation of this type of marriage in the little, small, daily, earthly matters. It's taking out the trash, picking up your dirty clothes, shutting off the game, making love when you're tired, stopping work to call, getting home on time, giving a neck rub, keeping your word, speaking words of grace in conflict, prioritizing cheap dates, and a thousand more. This lifestyle calls us to the cross.

The first communion in the upper room pointed forward to the cross. Ever since, each celebration of communion has looked back on the power of the cross. Consequently, when Paul writes about the mystical marriage between Christ and His bride (the Church), He appeals to this act of sacrifice in Ephesians 5:25: "Husbands, love your wives, just as Christ loved the church and gave himself up for her . . ."

Level 5 Marriage Characteristics

Self-sharing love. The love that marks your marriage is the self-sharing love that Christ demonstrated. Level 5 marriages live in the centrality of the cross. Few couples value the power of the cross highly enough. Few depend on its power to create communion in their relationship. Yet it's the grace, humility, mercy, perseverance, forgiveness, courage, and love found at the cross that bridge the gaps between us and intertwine our hearts together. The cross is the key to a Level 5 marriage and a Level 5 family. When couples reach this level in their marriage, the children benefit. When people live as merciful, forgiving, loving and patient, humble and courageous disciples, then these attitudinal attributes flow out to those in their orbits, including their children. These become "normal" behaviors in the home, in contrast to homes where conflict and selfishness seem "normal."

Deb and I chose communion as the first act of our married lives together. Before the dance, before the cake, before the toast, before the introduction to the congregation, even before the kiss, we shared communion. I took the bread and cup and served it to her, and then she served me. This was a bold declaration to ourselves, the church, and to Satan that our marriage found its life and power in the cross of Jesus. It also was a statement of the mission of our marriage. We had not come together just for what it could offer us but so our marriage could offer the power of the cross to many others. We knew we desired intimacy and impact.

Self-giving intimacy. Sexual intimacy is God's physical picture of interpersonal communion in marriage. The world preaches that sex is a way to take pleasure for yourself. Every man and woman for themselves. God's design is to give pleasure to your spouse, and then you receive pleasure, as well. In this "self-giving," that satisfying sexual interaction occurs. It is a holistic giving, not merely physical.

We believe one reason our culture is sex-crazed is because every person has an internal yearning to return to the Garden and to the wonder of being "naked and unashamed," fully vulnerable, secure, and loved. Lacking the truth of the gospel and the grace of God, our culture substitutes physical nakedness and sexual intimacy. But God's version of sexual intimacy is a giving of body, soul, and spirit in a communion based on monogamous, lifelong commitment. Level 5 marriages understand and enjoy this type of intimacy.

Self-giving communication. The words "communion" and "communication" are inextricably linked. You do not achieve a communion marriage without becoming excellent communicators with each other. Level 5 marriages understand that every marriage rises or falls on the quality of their communication. Great communication in itself is "self-giving" in every interaction.

Effective listening is a combination of attitude and skill. You care enough to learn the art of listening. You care enough to make it a daily habit. Intent listening isn't hearing words but rather listening to the heart of your spouse. Level 5 marriages have helped one another understand their hearts (emotions, feelings, fears, dreams, yearnings) and assisted each other in articulating the heart so these "heart realities" could be shared together.

Self-deflecting ministry. In Level 5 marriages, the ministry has become a natural outflow of the love and values you share as a couple. Ministry is not only something you do; it's also an intrinsic part of who you are together. You champion them, pray for them, resource them, and cheer for them. You know and honor your spouse's gifts. You rejoice when they rejoice and weep when they weep. You flow in and out of each other's specific ministries, sparking spiritual and ministerial passion in one another.

At Level 5, your goals don't primarily focus on growing your ministry or church but on multiplying new disciples, ministries and churches. Christian stardom or the legacy of your name are no longer enamoring. Your ministries revolve around, "making disciples who make disciples." You invite others into your lives not to impress them but to imprint them with Kingdom DNA. Your marriage communion is so Christ-centered that you birth spiritual children who want to follow your example and so do your biological ones. Together, you make heroes of others. You're fruitful, and you multiply.

Level 5 marriages don't grow simply through determination but much like a fine wine, they age into maturity. The process of exploring each other's intricate design, observing the shaping work of the Spirit in your spouse, dying to our inherent selfishness, and learning the songs of each other's hearts—these take devotion, Spirit-reliance and time. This is the splendor of a Level 5 marriage. Author Eugene Peterson once said that discipleship is obedience in the same direction (and wrote a book of the same name). We could say that a Level 5 marriage is a long devotion in the same direction..

But how do you build a flourishing marriage and family? We believe there are five essential habits. Are you ready to commit to and move toward Level 5?

CHAPTER 3

Habit 1

The Humility You Practice

"Submit to one another out of reverence for Christ."
Ephesians 5:21

*"Do you wish to rise? Begin by descending.
You plan a tower that will pierce the clouds?
Lay first the foundation of humility."*
—Saint Augustine

The mayor of a small town and his wife returned to their hometown for their twenty-fifth high school reunion. One of his wife's old boyfriends was valeting the cars—the same work he had been doing twenty-five years earlier. Later that night, the mayor smugly remarked, "Honey, just think: If you hadn't married me, you'd be married to a car valet." To which she replied, "Honey, if I had married him, he would have been the mayor."

We build a Level 5 marriage by correctly understanding humility and actively practicing it in our marriage relationship. We can help one another become who God intends us to be, but not if we allow pride to creep in and corrupt our thinking. Few of us think of ourselves as proud, showing once again that deception is the first ingredient of pride.

People tend to think that what will transport them to a blissful marriage is practicing a few marriage skills and a few good daily behaviors. But what we've seen in both our marriage and others' marriages is that the habits that matter most are those of the heart, the habitual attitudes with which we approach marriage. If you want marriage tricks, go see a magician. If you want marriage transformation, go see the heart surgeon. Habits of the heart will produce the relationship you really want, and humility is perhaps the most influential.

Humility in the Five Levels of Marriage

Level 1: A Level 1 marriage lives in the muck of obvious pride. They show little concern for their mate except when it will help them get their own way. They are consumers. One or both spouses live in unconcealed selfishness and self-justification. "I'm sorry," is rarely spoken. Their self-reliance manifests itself in little or no prayer.

Level 2: Level 2 marriages have less apparent forms of pride. They serve their spouse when it's convenient. They feel self-reflection or counseling is a waste of time and want convenience more than change. They are nitpicky, finding their spouse's faults with little recognition of their own. They assign blame easily, seldom seeking God for themselves or their marriage.

Level 3: Level 3 marriages have some level of value for humility. They want to have less pride but not if it means a deep dive into their own patterns of behavior. They are committed to God, to each other, and to improving their marriage. However, they tend to rely on doing the right things rather than leaning fully into the power of God. They are often motivated by a desire to have the appearance of success. They want a better marriage as long as it fits into their ministry agenda.

Level 4: Level 4 marriages place a high value on practicing humility. This manifests as daily habits of concern for their spouse and their needs. Prayer for their marriage is a valued practice. Each spouse actively looks for ways to sacrificially serve each other. Ministry must shape itself around the priority of their marriage. They are more concerned about character than success. Their humility empowers them to work together without concern for who gets the applause.

Level 5: Level 5 marriages are lived by two individuals who have allowed the Spirit to break them deeply. Their communion in marriage is shaped by the extreme kindness they manifest to each other in small and large ways. They would rather see their spouse honored than themselves. Prayerful dependence upon God is the daily oxygen.

The First Marriage Fail

Adam and Eve were enjoying a perfect marriage, working together in God's garden, eating the fruit of the trees. Enjoying the beauties of creation. Walking with God in the cool of the day. It was all as God designed until sin disrupted their union. It was the same attitude and action that had led to the first sin in the universe. In his heart, Lucifer said, "I will make myself like the Most High" (Isa. 14:14). Now, here in the Garden, he spread his disease into the hearts of Adam and Eve (Gen. 3:5). Perhaps Eve thought God was holding something good back from them or that He was keeping them in the dark about their own "divine potential." They, too, could be gods. Rather than living in dependency upon God, they could be equals with God. Choosing the lie of pride caused her to bite the bad fruit. Adam eagerly joined her.

The same pride that had led to Lucifer's fall led to theirs. The consequences for their marriage were immediate and profound. Their intimacy and vulnerability were damaged. They experienced shame and insecurity. They invented the "blame game," and the hiding started. The masks appeared. The curse of sin brought inequality to the relationship (Gen. 3:16). Shared dominion was replaced by domination and subjugation.

The contamination from the fall is a present reality every couple must deal with daily. The temptation that deceived the original couple is the same one we must battle—our own pride, our desire to be self-centered and self-reliant, our tendency to live independent of God and one another. Proverbs 16:18 is a red warning light on the dashboard of our marriages: "Pride goes before destruction, a haughty spirit before a fall." Only the power of the cross, walking in the Spirit, and dying to self daily can overcome its insidious downward pull.

Wes was a confident and competent leader. He was often the smartest person in the room. His wife, Kris, was also quite capable, although Wes left little space for her when they were in public together. Wes was zealous for God, for ministry—and himself. Nevertheless, their marriage seemed quite solid and we watched Wes' ministry grow. As his reputation grew, his spiritual guard dropped. A subtle narcissism crept into his approach to his marriage. Kris, confusing acquiescence with humility and finding her own status in her husband's ministry, stayed in her corner rather than confronting what was becoming more apparent. One day, Kris came to Deb tearfully. She had found Wes' cell phone filled with nude photos of him and another woman in the church. Wes' pride was up, but his zipper was down.

Playing Defense

Unless we live in the recognition of the danger *and* the realization of God's overcoming power, we will fail to build an effective ministry marriage. This is why God admonishes us in Proverbs 4:23: "Above all else, guard your heart, for everything you do flows from it." Your heart is like a well the enemy is seeking to contaminate. Your marriage relationship flows from the purity of your heart. Pride poisons the well.

The promise to your marriage is John 10:10: "The thief comes only to steal and kill and destroy; I have come that they may have life, and have it to the full." God's intention for our marriage is that it flourish and be full, but we must stand guard against the thief. That's where humility comes in. It's the effective defense against the liar. Grace is the clarion call of James 4:6-7: "God opposes the proud but shows favor to the humble. Submit yourselves, then, to God. Resist the devil, and he will flee from you."

Pride will not impact most marriages in the manner it did Wes and Kris. Pride's poison will usually be subtler, not killing the marriage but keeping it from full health. Over the years, we've learned to identify five significant ways the pursuit of humility builds an influential marriage.

Five Reasons Why Practicing Humility Grows a Level 5 Marriage

#1 "It is from Him, through Him and to Him!" (Rom. 11:36).

- Our marriage is *from* Him. Our marriage is not about us—at least in the sense that "us" is not the starting point. God is. Accepting our marriage as a gift of God's grace rather than a work we've achieved positions us to daily give thanks for this privilege of being married to our spouse. We challenged one wife who had lost her desire for her husband to start and end each day by thanking God for three things her husband was or did that day. The practice humbled her as she realized the gift of their marriage.
- Our marriage is *through* Him. Living in absolute daily dependence upon His power and wisdom to defend and build our marriage aligns us for God's divine assistance. Every great marriage starts with the declaration, "I can't!" *I can't be the husband or wife my spouse needs.* But it quickly follows the first declaration with a second, "I can!" *As I team up today with God, I can be who God wants me to be and who my spouse needs me to be in this marriage.*

- Our marriage is *to* Him. Making our marriage an act of worship to direct positive attention toward God positions us to experience God's favor. Our top priority in marriage is not our pleasure but God's glory. We conduct our marriage as a sacrifice of praise to bless God.

The more we mature in this humble understanding of our marriage, the softer the clay of our marriage becomes. The more valuable vessel the sculptor can create out of our marriage. Sadly, I have heard different teachers exclaim, "The husband is the head, the wife is the neck. The mission of the neck is to lift up the head." The biblical truth is that the husband and wife are one, a part of the body of Christ. The body has one primary mission, to lift up the true head, Jesus. Our marriages can be the best or worst advertisements for how amazing Jesus is.

Our friends, Stuart and Teresa McKnight, pastor a large church in Canada and are raising six amazing children. Having spent time in their home on various occasions, Deb and I have had a front-row seat to their marriage. Repeatedly, we have been struck by how grounded, authentic and loving their relationship is. Both are on a quest to build up the other and to see their spouse's desires realized. Stuart is an expert on the Trinity, teaching on the subject with a stunning clarity and applicability. We glimpse the Trinitarian unity in their marriage, the key ingredient being humility. They see their marriage "from him, through him and to Him."

#2 *"It's not about a "little me," but rather a "big God."*

Frequently, we tend to confuse humility with inferiority. Thinking critically, negatively or dismissively of ourselves tries to pass itself off as humility. If we discount ourselves while embellishing others, we wrongly believe we're on the path of humility. When John the Baptist made his famous statement in John 3:30, "He must increase and I must decrease," he wasn't belittling himself. He was confident in who he was and what God had called him to do. He understood that his mission was to increase the reputation of Jesus, not make one for himself.

We've all heard the adage, "Humility is not thinking less of yourself; it is thinking of yourself less." Pride is a preoccupation with yourself; humility is a self-forgetfulness. What engenders such a "self-forgetfulness" is a confidence in who God has made you. When you believe you're a masterpiece with a mission only you can do (Eph. 2:10); when you trust that nothing can separate you from the love of God in Christ Jesus (Rom. 8:39); when you're convinced that God will finish the good work He has begun in your life (Phil. 1:6); *then* you can operate in the beauty of the security of humility. You can rise to your full potential without wallowing in the world's opinions of you.

Deb and I know a wife in our church who has lived under the stifling lie of low self-esteem. This woman has attempted to increase her "value" in a number of ways—through pursuing accomplishments, overhauling her appearance, isolating herself, critiquing others and much therapy. All to no avail. As a result, this high-potential marriage is now hanging on by a few shreds of commitment. Her battle is with pride—the type of pride that refuses to believe God's truth about her.

In a Level 5 marriage, humility manifests itself in a security about who you are without your spouse. Each spouse has come to understand themselves so keenly in God that they're not reliant on their spouse's opinion for their self-worth or identity. They know themselves in God. Their humility welcomes God's grace and secures their hearts. Consequently, they have a wonderful person to freely offer to their spouse.

We also tend to confuse humility with fear. Humility is not denying your strengths. It's being honest about your weaknesses. Each of us is a bundle of great strengths and great weaknesses; humility is the vulnerability to be honest about both. Paul was able to say, "Follow me as I follow Christ," and, "I'm the chief among sinners." In humility, he could write down his weaknesses without caving in to fear. God wants us to be humble, but He does not want us to be fearful. To accomplish less than what God desires is not humility, but fear.

#3 *"It's about my plank, not her/his speck!"*

I've often heard people point out that pride is always an "I" problem. Others have noted that both "sin" and "pride" have a big "I" in the middle. Jesus referred to the human pride problem when he asked the question in Luke 6:41-42: "Why do you look at the speck of sawdust in your brother's eye and pay no attention to the plank in your own eye? How can you say to your brother, 'Brother, let me take the speck out of your eye,' when you yourself fail to see the plank in your own eye? You hypocrite, first take the plank out of your eye, and then you will see clearly to remove the speck from your brother's eye."

Jesus teaches us that pride misplaces our focus. It moves us to focus on the shortcomings of others. Pride distorts your vision of yourself, allowing you to miss seeing the plank in your own actions, attitudes, words, or motives. It blocks self-awareness. This practice in a marriage is the potent force of destruction.

Healthy individuals understand the power of self-awareness. In his powerful book, **Practicing Greatness**, author Reggie McNeal believes this is a discipline necessary for great leadership. "The single most important piece of information the leader possesses is self-awareness," he writes. He goes on to explain this discipline includes self-knowledge, self-vigilance, self-consciousness, and self-alertness, which provide us the road markers for self-evaluation.[1]

Self-awareness changes the climate of a team (or marriage). Daniel Goleman, the researcher and author who popularized the concept of emotional intelligence cites the work of the Korn Ferry Hay Group. This research group found that among leaders with multiple strengths in emotional self-awareness, ninety-two percent had teams with high energy and high performance. In sharp contrast, leaders low in emotional self-awareness created negative climates seventy-eight percent of the time. If this is true in teams at work, then it is even more influential in the marriage and home.[2]

Lack of self-awareness is usually some form of defensiveness rooted in pride. My stepdad battled an anger problem. He often spoke to my mother with words and a tone of voice I hated. I swore to myself I would never, ever sound that way to my wife. The rest of this story will not surprise you if you understand the shaping power of your family of origin.

Deb and I had been married for two years, and she started to confront me about the way I spoke to her at times.

"You are hurting me," she said. "You sound just like your stepdad."

"There is no way," I responded. "You're just being overly sensitive. I don't sound like him at all!"

A few months later, I had been recording for a teaching I was doing. Deb had come in the room, and we had a heated discussion. I didn't realize the recorder was still on. When I listened to our conversation, I was devastated. I heard my stepdad in my voice. I heard the belittling, disrespectful tone. To this day, I get teary-eyed thinking about it. My pride had blocked my self-awareness. One of the prayers Deb and I pray frequently is, "Lord, tell me the truth about me."

One of the tools we have adapted and incorporated into our relationship is the Johari Window. This tool, created by Joseph Luft and Harrington Ingham in 1955 is based on the idea that we have four panes in the window of our lives:

1. The Open – What we know and what we show to others;
2. The Façade – What we know but what we don't show to others;
3. The Blind Spot – What others know but what we don't know about ourselves;
4. The Unknown – What we and others don't know.

In the Unknown quadrant, Deb and I would assert that *God* knows and desires to reveal our lives to us. In our opinion, the larger our "Open" pane grows, the more self-aware and the freer we are in life. We see accurately, and we have nothing to hide.

Consequently, we want each other to share what they see in us that we don't see in ourselves. God tells us, "Wounds from a friend can be trusted" (Prov. 27:6). My spouse is my friend. Humility invites these trustworthy corrections. Notice Jesus doesn't say in Luke 6:41-42 that we should not help one another remove their specks. He does say, "Start with your own 'stuff' first."

Conversely, true humility is proactive in being a "good-finder" instead of a "speck-finder." Whether it's not enough sex, the dirty dishes, his belching, her tardiness in leaving for parties or spending too much money, complaints are inevitable in any marriage. The question is whether the couple is majoring in compliments or complaints.

To understand the difference between happy and unhappy couples, Dr. Gottman and Robert Levenson began doing longitudinal studies of couples in the 1970s. They asked couples to solve a conflict in their relationship in fifteen minutes, then sat back and watched. After carefully reviewing the tapes and following up with these marriages nine years later, they were able to predict with more than ninety percent accuracy which couples would stay together and which would divorce.

Their discovery was simple. The difference between happy and unhappy couples is the balance between positive and negative interactions during conflict. There is a very specific ratio that makes love last. That "magic ratio" is 5:1, meaning that for every negative interaction during conflict, a stable and happy marriage has five (or more) positive interactions.[3]

The other aspect of seeing your own plank first is the humility to apologize sincerely and quickly. You can often gauge the pride level in a marriage by how easily and deeply a spouse can respond, "I am so sorry. Please forgive me." When a misunderstanding, disappointment, hurt, or conflict happens, humility and grace need to rush in to heal the wound. When self-defense, rationalization, or minimization are the response, then healing is delayed.

The more mature your marriage is, the easier you recognize when a look, action, or word has hurt your spouse. You exercise repentance before even being asked. But also the spouse who is offended humbles themselves to respond with grace. Rather than punishing the offender or making him or her grovel for a time, the offended spouse releases them with words of absolution: "Thank you for your apology. I forgive you. Can we discuss how to avoid this in the future?"

#4 "It's not about my needs; it's about her/his needs!"

The denial of our own needs is not the path to a Level 5 marriage. In fact, denial of our own needs creates a "doormat marriage," in which the spouse in power wipes their feet on the other spouse. Meanwhile, the doormat spouse interprets their weakness as "dying to self" for the sake of the marriage. Humility is not ignorance nor rejection of our own needs. *Humility is deciding to prioritize the needs of our spouse first while practicing healthy self-care.* It's living in a daily posture of servanthood.

Philippians 2:3-4 says, "Do nothing from selfish ambition or conceit, but in humility count others more significant than yourselves. Let each of you look not only to his own interests, but also to the interests of others" (ESV). This isn't a renunciation of your needs or interests but rather a humility seeking first to serve over being served.

Jesus models this priority. He served the needs of the people, yet often left the crowds to care for His own needs of spiritual solitude and replenishment. Self-care is essential to serving your spouse and others well. The problem lies in our common insistence to serve ourselves first.

The old tale of the banquet table with abnormally long spoons is too true when we apply it to humility in marriage. There was a banquet table loaded with all types of delicious spoonable foods in the center of the table. At each place setting was an abnormally long-handled spoon, prohibiting anyone from getting food into their mouth. The trick was to realize that the joy of the banquet comes from feeding your neighbor. Insist on selfishly feeding yourself, and you'll starve. Use your spoon to help your partner, and you'll feast.

One father of three bragged to me, "I never change a dirty diaper. My job is to pay for the diapers so she can change them." I just shook my head. If I had been quicker-witted, I would have responded, "Jesus made the disciples feet, but He washed them, too." Humility runs to serve. It looks for opportunities not to be served but to serve. Level 5 marriages flourish with abundance because couples wake up thinking, *How can I bless and serve my spouse today?*

Level 5 marriages have developed a habit of striving to make life better for their spouse. This flows into ministry as well, as the couple exemplifies what it means to serve their congregation, followers and staff. Loving servant leadership is the norm, flowing from a humble heart seeking to bless others and ultimately, to please God.

#5 *"We are partners, not competitors!"*

Writing in his seminal work, *Mere Christianity*, author C.S. Lewis says, "Pride gets no pleasure out of having something, only out of having more of it than the next man . . . It is the comparison that makes you proud: the pleasure of being above the rest. Once the element of competition is gone, pride is gone."[4]

We can apply Lewis' wisdom to our marriages. Read the words Deb so transparently shares on this point:

"Have you ever struggled with keeping your mouth shut when your spouse gets honored for what really was your work? The temptation is to blurt correctives in attempts to set the record straight. Working together as a ministry couple can get convoluted. We have found in our marriage that the more prominent leader gets the kudos while the spouse takes solace in the fact their heavenly crown will have more jewels one day. These types of frustrations are not uncommon in a marriage, especially if it's a ministry marriage. Practicing humility is a critical habit to help move marriages to Level 5 where you are partners rather than competitors.

"I struggled with this a few years back. I went through a season of struggle as I wallowed in desperation to find my place as a leader called by God to the Church. For about eighteen months, there was a negative vibe in our marriage, exacerbated by my insecurity. People often do not ascribe insecurity as an expression of pride, but it is. Pride continually points back to self, thus giving rise to insecurity.

"A person struggling with this issue experiences consuming thoughts: *Am I good enough? Why won't people recognize me? Am I invisible? Does God really have something He wants me to do on this mission with Him?* The internal dialogue or self-talk of self-doubt is endless. The focus remains on self until something breaks the bondage.

"The difficulty for me as a female leader and pastor is living in Larry's shadow for much of our marriage. Over the years, Larry has been recognized on many levels as a pastor and leader, sought after for speaking, consulting, teaching, and coaching. Unfortunately, my insecure struggles pushed me toward isolation and an eventual, "dark night of the soul" journey. During that time, I questioned my leadership calling and created a self-imposed silencing of my leadership voice.

"My drift into depression caused a conflictual tenor in our relationship. The more recognition Larry received, the deeper I swirled into a pit of despair. At the darkest point of my journey, I decided I was not called into ministry but to only serve my husband and family. Deep down, I knew that was "stinkin' thinkin'" but just couldn't find the courage to ask for help.

"Feeling helpless, Larry prayed for me, but he didn't know how to coach me through my pain. God heard my pleas, and after eighteen months passed, He broke the lies I had spun. At a leadership retreat, He spoke clearly and precisely to my heart, calling me to pursue my leadership gift. With tears and repentance, the slow trek out of the abyss began. Today, I can easily declare that God wants me to be a leader of leaders. I choose to say yes to that call.

"Does insecurity ever raise its nasty head? Yes, many times. But in humility, I choose to not listen to its deceit. I choose to accept the roles God has chosen for me while applauding and cheering for Larry and all God has called him to do. Choosing to lay down my pride each time I sense the shaking of my confidence leads me back to the mind of Christ."

What a vulnerable example of how comparison can hobble a marriage and ministry. Watching Deb walk though this season, I realized I had contributed to her struggle. I sought forgiveness but also continue to seek to learn where my pride pushes myself up and others down.

Crafting a Level 5 marriage begins with the humility of mind that Jesus demonstrated and taught. The Kingdom mission is crying out for marriages humble enough to be truly one, humble enough to joyfully serve, humble enough to live in God-reliance, humble enough to be good-finders, humble enough to partner without seeking the spotlight, and humble enough to give their marriage away to others.

Assessment: Practicing Humility

Using the following scale with each question, rate your marriage 1 to 5 on each of these statements:

1. We are sensitive to the deceptive power of pride and actively ask God for humility.

1	2	3	4	5
Almost Never	Seldom	Frequently	Usually	Almost Always

2. We view our marriage as God's gift and thank Him for it often.

1	2	3	4	5
Almost Never	Seldom	Frequently	Usually	Almost Always

3. The quality of our marriage is an effective witness for the power of the gospel.

1	2	3	4	5
Almost Never	Seldom	Frequently	Usually	Almost Always

4. Each of us is secure in who we are in God and doesn't require our spouse's approval to feel valuable.

1	2	3	4	5
Almost Never	Seldom	Frequently	Usually	Almost Always

5. We understand the basics of emotional intelligence and pursue self-awareness as a key to our personal growth.

1	2	3	4	5
Not true at all	Somewhat True	Basically True	True	Very True

6. We are "good-finders" with our ratio of compliments to critiques being 5:1 or better.

1	2	3	4	5
Almost Never	Seldom	Frequently	Usually	Almost Always

7. We are sensitive to our "blind spots" and actively seek to open the window of our lives more fully to live more transparently.

1	2	3	4	5
Almost Never	Seldom	Frequently	Usually	Almost Always

8. We are quick to sincerely apologize when we have hurt each other, and we offer grace to one another easily.

1	2	3	4	5
Almost Never	Seldom	Frequently	Usually	Almost Always

9. We share household, parenting and life chores mutually, actively seeking how we can serve one another more effectively.

1	2	3	4	5
Almost Never	Seldom	Frequently	Usually	Almost Always

10. We refuse to compare ourselves or compete with one another. Instead, we partner to help each other be their best.

1	2	3	4	5
Almost Never	Seldom	Frequently	Usually	Almost Always

CHAPTER 4

Habit 2
Spiritually Engaged

". . . For where two or three gather in my name, there am I with them."
(Matt. 18:20)

"I love you not only for what you are, but for what I am when I am with you. I love you not only for what you have made of yourself, but for what you are making of me."
—Roy Croft

- -

I often jokingly tell people, "Deb and I lived together before we were married." The truth is I invited four of my college friends to spend the summer with my family in our big Kansas farm house. We would work on the farm during the week and spend weekends ministering as a singing and preaching group around the area. Deb played the keys and sang. I preached. We had been dating, and our feelings for each other were growing stronger by the week.

The final event of our summer ministry was a large youth camp where I was the main speaker. The camp organizers had given me a small trailer to use for preparing my sermons and prayer. As the final service of the camp drew near, I was in the trailer writing and praying for those at the camp who didn't know Christ. I became so emotional thinking about these kids that my tears blurred the ink on the sermon manuscript I was working on.

Meanwhile, Deb had sensed she needed to find me and be with me. Quietly, she opened the trailer door, walked in, placed her hands on my shoulders and began to pray. Within the minute, her heart joined mine, and her own tears also began to fall. Looking back, I realize we were sharing God's heart together. At the risk of sounding melodramatic, it was that moment I decided she was absolutely the woman I wanted to marry. The next day she said, "Yes!"

Deb has been my prayer warrior for more than forty years. Every time I preach, she's praying. Likewise, when she preaches, I'm on the front row praying. As important as our intercessory prayers for each other are, the more essential prayers are our prayers together. These spiritual interactions are life to our marriage. While few of our interactions have been as poignant as that day in the trailer, each small sharing in Christ together strengthens our lives and marriage.

Spiritual engagement creates thriving marriages.

The most fulfilling type of oneness in a marriage is spiritual unity. Yet the most neglected aspect of most ministry marriages is vital and habitual spiritual engagement. The excuses are many: "We're too busy. When the kids get older. I pray for him/her on my own. I feel awkward praying with him/her. I don't know how to engage spiritually. We do our own devotions. I pray better alone. There's too much hurt, or disappointment, or insecurity, or comparison to share spiritual times together. We have different spiritual temperaments. We're wired differently. We have different expectations."

While some of these excuses may be true, none are important enough to inhibit or block sharing your lives with Jesus and with each other.

Spiritual Engagement in the Five Levels of Marriage

Level 1: A Level 1 marriage has little to no spiritual engagement with one another. Couples don't prioritize the pursuit of spiritual matters.

Spouses may be in church or small group together, but their spirits are not joining together to worship or pray. Any devotional life is carried out individually.

Level 2: A Level 2 marriage has some spiritual engagement, but it's mostly religious in nature and sporadic more than disciplined. If they're not convenient, couples avoid spiritual disciplines. They may occasionally pray "for" one another but seldom "with" one another.

Level 3: A Level 3 marriage is often fairly faithful in devotional life together. There is some sharing of spiritual learnings. Their zeal for their church or ministry helps them pray with one another, but it rarely goes into deep prayer for one another. The presence of the Spirit is an afterthought more than the first thought of their day together.

Level 4: A Level 4 marriage has moved into a thorough integration of spiritual life into the daily fabric of life and marriage. Couples employ and enjoy spiritual practices both individually and together. They have an understanding of each other's spiritual temperament and a desire to support each other in it. They frequently share what God is doing and saying.

Level 5: A Level 5 marriage has matured into an overflowing spiritual well. This marriage reflects habitual communion with the Spirit of God and with the spirit of their spouse. They share in Jesus together. They relish in individual, couple, and corporate worship times. People often comment on how naturally and thoroughly Jesus is woven into their relationship. They want the spiritual unity they see in this couple. This communion is, of course, unperfected and at times interrupted by weaknesses and life's distractions. But it has become the normal default state of life.

The "With Christ" Marriage

Deb and I have often been troubled by how little attention couples give to the development of a flourishing love life with Jesus. If our marriage is to reflect Christ, then He must be the first pursuit of our marriage. As Deb says, "People need to see a life *with* Christ, not just *for* Christ!" We must immerse our marriages in Christ and then do ministry from that place of Spirit-empowered intimacy.

Some of the best marriage advice I ever received was captured in two words: "Include Jesus." Whatever you're doing, "include Jesus." Good times, bad times, fun times, play times, work times, tired, hungry, feasting, vacation, happy, scared, argument, love making—"include Jesus." The idea is to make the presence of Jesus natural, pervasive, and endemic to all you do instead of sequestering Him to devotional times, Sunday worship, and prayers before meals. When Jesus is included, you laugh deeper, love more passionately, and your fears are smaller. "Including Jesus" means treating Him like He's there because He has promised that when two are gathered in His name (Matt. 18:20), He's present . . . so include Him.

The "One Another" Marriage

To put some practical handles on spiritual engagement, we suggest you focus on the "one anothers" in your marriage. The New Testament includes fifty-nine "one another" verses that tell us we should act, think or speak to another brother or sister in a certain manner. Deb and I believe the "one anothers" start in the home with our spouse. To repeat ourselves and paraphrase Paul, "practice at home what you want to see practiced in the church" (1 Tim. 3:5). When you devote yourself to the "one anothers" in your marriage, your marriage begins to be shaped by Scripture's influence.

Consider just a few of these admonitions: Pray for one another. Encourage one another. Bear with one another. Confess your sins to one another. Forgive one another. Instruct one another. Build up one another. Serve one another. Don't grumble against one another. Submit to one another. Carry one another's burden. Then my favorite, "Greet one another with a kiss." If couples practiced these each day, it would revolutionize marriages.

When we determine to pursue spiritual intimacy in our marriages, we position ourselves for the ongoing infilling of the Holy Spirit. Ephesians 5:18 says, "Do not get drunk on wine, which leads to debauchery. Instead, be filled with the Spirit . . ." The Greek carries the idea of "being filled with the Spirit" as in make this a daily practice. Our marriages cannot overflow unless we're filled both individually and as a couple with the Spirit's presence.

Most people erroneously stop their thought at the end of Ephesians 5:18 in the middle of Paul's sentence. What follows is both an avenue for being filled with the Spirit and a result of the Spirit's infilling. Paul goes on to say, ". . . speaking to one another with psalms, hymns, and songs from the Spirit. Sing and make music from your heart to the Lord, always giving thanks to God the Father for everything, in the name of our Lord Jesus Christ" (Eph. 5:19-20).

Did you see the light Paul shares here? There is a "one-anotherness" to this infilling. When we "speak to one another" in spiritual words and gifts; when we make heartfelt spiritual music in our marriage; when we continually express gratitude to God in our marriage; when the name of our Lord Jesus Christ is habitually glorified in our marriage; *then* we experience this ongoing flow of the Spirit. People begin to see a marriage done "with" Christ, not just "for" Him.

My sister and brother-in-law, Brenda and Mark Williams, could not be more different personalities. She was a beauty pageant queen raised in Sunday school, and he was a long-haired, Harley Davidson-rider who grew up in his parents' bar. My parents and our relatives were shocked when they were married. Their saving grace was they had both made a profound commitment to Jesus as Lord. Over the years, Deb and I have observed and learned from Mark and Brenda's marriage.

We both say we don't know a more spiritually engaged couple than them. Every morning, they get up before sunrise to seek God individually and together. Their prayer lists are legendary. Their Bibles are falling apart from overuse. They take their conflicts literally to the cross. The result? They have spiritually impacted hundreds of lives. They also lead a large support and recovery ministry to help the hurting, addicted and poor. A flourishing, authentic life of the Spirit flows from them. While Brenda has a gifted singing voice, Mark can't carry a tune in a bucket. Yet often, you'll hear them heartily singing worship songs as they do their chores together.

Ordinary Moments Spirituality

A Level 5 marriage is marked by disciplined spiritual times but even more by "ordinary moments of the day"-type of prayer and worship. Although he isn't writing specifically about marriage, in his watershed book, *The Divine Conspiracy*, author and theologian Dallas Willard describes prayer in a way that captures the essence of the natural flow of spiritual engagement (italics mine):

> "Accordingly, I believe the most adequate description of prayer is simply, 'Talking to God about what we are doing together.' That immediately focuses the activity where we are but at the same time drives the egotism out of it. Requests will naturally be made in the course of this conversational walk. Prayer is *a matter of explicitly sharing with God my concerns about what He too is concerned about in my life.* And of course He is concerned about my concerns and, in particular, that my concerns should coincide with His. This is our walk together. Out of it I pray.[1]

Our marriages must learn to integrate this "talking to God about what we are doing together" and talking with our spouse about what God is doing today. Often Deb will share something the Spirit has just shared with her from the Word, or something God is convicting her about, or a burden God is placing on her heart for someone, or a new ministry dream she's beginning to have. I try to do the same. Often we stop and pray in the moment about these.

Sharing Spiritual Disciplines

When I decided to return to school for my doctorate, I was anxious to focus on church leadership and church growth. I am a type A, achiever, activator kind of leader, and I wanted to further develop my ability to excel in specific areas. But the Holy Spirit, partly through Deb, checked me on this: Could my pursuit of performing better be leading me to a shallow spirituality? Would I (and our marriage and ministry) benefit more if I sought a doctorate that emphasized deepening my spiritual well? I knew very little about the classic spiritual disciplines, and that weakness was hindering my spiritual life. I ended up enrolling in a Doctorate of Ministry program stressing spiritual formation. While my propensity towards busyness is still a challenge, this choice has made me a different Christ follower.

Understanding and practicing the spiritual disciplines together is the life blood of a spiritually engaged marriage. Few Christian marriages take the classic spiritual disciplines seriously enough.

In our marriage, these twelve disciplines have been vital:

1. Prayer – communicating with God.
2. Meditation – focusing on God, His Word, His will.
3. Fasting – abstaining from food or sex to more intensely seek God.
4. Study – gaining insights into spiritual truth through research and learning.

5. Simplicity – finding ways to reduce the clutter in our lives and our possessions.
6. Submission – yielding ourselves to God, each other, and spiritual leaders.
7. Solitude – withdrawing from the world to spend time alone with God.
8. Service – serving those in need, especially anonymously.
9. Confession – acknowledging our sin to God, to each other and to close spiritual friends.
10. Guidance – receiving direction from wise counsel for the sake of our lives, our ministry, and our marriage.
11. Celebration – taking joy in what God has done.
12. Worship – giving God glory through our attitudes and actions.

Spiritual engagement may take various forms. They can be momentary and spontaneous, planned and disciplined, simple and daily, or lengthy and detailed. Deb and I still fall short in the level of spiritual interaction we hope to have, but we love our shared life of spiritual formation. To help you think practically, we share some specific examples of spiritual engagement that are meaningful to us.

1. Reading the same daily passage of the Bible and discussing what God is saying to us.
2. Journaling thoughts and prayers and sharing some of them with each other.
3. Taking turns praying before meals and really praying for our lives, not just our food.
4. Reading spiritual books and discussing what we're learning.
5. Fasting together.
6. Interceding for a particular need together.
7. Singing worship together in the car or at home.
8. Listening to Christian radio together.
9. Taking communion in church together.
10. Praying together during our morning devotions.

11. Driving along and suddenly praying aloud about something on our hearts.
12. Discussing theology together.
13. Laying hands on each other to pray for healing.
14. Sharing in the beauty of creation together and bursting out in praise.
15. Doing random acts of kindness together in Jesus' name.
16. Singing loudly in church as we worship with the saints.
17. Taking a spiritual retreat for prayer.
18. Spending half a day silent in each other's presence.
19. Filling our shared office with praise music.
20. Discussing sacrificial financial gifts to the ministry.
21. Reading the same chapter of Proverbs each day and discussing it.
22. Prayer walking in our neighborhood.
23. Carrying out anonymous love missions to hurting people.
24. Emailing each other verses or spiritual quotes.
25. Walking in silence watching the sunrise.
26. Holding hands during worship.
27. Going forward to be prayed for by our prayer team during service.
28. Providing hospitality or lodging to travelers who visit our church.
29. Attending a spiritual formation class, seminar or conference together.
30. Confessing our sins to one another and receiving prayer.

Your Spouse's Spiritual Temperament

One helpful resource for our marriage has been the work by author Gary Thomas on the different spiritual temperaments and how they help us understand how our spouse might best connect with God. In his book, *Nine Spiritual Temperaments*, Thomas identifies at least nine distinct spiritual temperaments that determine how an individual best worships and relates to God. See if you can recognize yourself (and your spouse) in one or more of the following:

- **Naturalists'** hearts open up to God when they get outdoors. God seems more real to them when they're hiking under a big expanse of sky or sitting under a tree.
- **Intellectuals** really like books—even reference titles—and live in the world of concepts. They want to come out of their devotional time with new understanding. If their mind isn't engaged, their heart may feel cold.
- **Sensates** are more aesthetically inclined. These are the artistic types, and they prefer creative and original music or even good architecture to open their hearts to God's presence. Their worship is about seeing, hearing, feeling, touching and even tasting God's presence.
- **Traditionalists** find great meaning by worshiping God, according to set patterns—their own or historical ones. They may organize their life around scheduled times of prayer and may even choose to carefully observe the Christian calendar, aligning themselves with centuries of faith. Traditionalists often make good use of Christian symbols.
- **Ascetics** meet God internally. They prefer to shut out the world and meet God in solitude and austerity. For ascetics, the best environment for personal worship is a quiet place with a rather orderly environment, and they usually don't like the distractions of group worship. They are often advocates of all-night prayer vigils and many of the classical disciplines, such as fasting and meditation.
- **Activists** meet God in the vortex of confrontation. They want to fight God's battles. God becomes most real to them when they're standing up for justice or working on the frontlines to build God's Kingdom.
- **Caregivers** love God by loving others. Providing care or meeting needs in Jesus' name spiritually energizes caregivers and draws them closer to the Lord.

- **Enthusiasts** like the excitement and celebration of group worship. They probably buy more praise music than books. They feed off the enthusiasm of other believers and typically revel in God's mystery and supernatural power. Their exuberance tends to lead them to embrace creative forms of worship.
- **Contemplatives** are marked by an emotional attachment and surrender to God. They are lovers of God, and they want to spend their time in His presence—adoring Him, listening to Him, and enjoying Him. They often find benefit in journal writing, where they can explore their heart's devotion.[2]

Honoring our spouse's spiritual temperament by growing in our appreciation and practice of their means of connecting with God can radically impact our depth of spiritual engagement. If you're not sure of your spiritual temperament (or your spouse's), we encourage you to spend time practicing each of them in your discovery process. Then spend time as a couple exploring each of them together. Trust us! What emerges from this will be helpful for the rest of your married lives.

Our Holiness Partner

Hebrews 3:13 gives us a command. We usually do not apply this scripture to marriage, but it actually should be the first place we practice it: "But encourage one another daily, as long as it is called 'Today,' so that none of you may be hardened by sin's deceitfulness." Sin's ability to deceive and harden our hearts is profound. Our spouse's encouragement in the direction of godliness can be an essential element in guarding our hearts.

One of the privileges of a spiritually engaged marriage is having someone close enough to warn you when you're in, or headed toward, sin. Deb will often admonish my bad attitude before it becomes a problem to my ministry. We give each other a standing invitation to identify and confront fallen thinking, selfish motives, fear-controlled decisions, people pleasing, lust-initiating environments, power-tripping, gossip, negativity, oversensitivity, and more.

Having the openness of a spiritual life that affords you the opportunity to confess your temptations to each other empowers each of you to avoid or overcome many of the enemy's tactics. For example, if a new woman starts attending our church, and I feel any form of attraction to her, I immediately share this with Deb so she can pray for me. To hide it or think I'm strong enough to ignore it is underestimating the enemy's power and withdrawing spiritually from Deb. Level 5 marriages are transparent with a view toward holiness of mind, motives, words, and actions.

Admittedly, Deb and I fall short of this call. Nevertheless, we take 1 Peter 1:15 seriously: "But just as he who called you is holy, so be holy in all you do . . ." This quest for holiness informs what we say "yes" to and what we avoid. We say "no" to certain pleasures, people, entertainment, situations, purchases, vocabulary, topics or media. Occasionally other Christians have critiqued us as legalistic, but we know we're simply seeking to obey what the Spirit leads us to do.

For example, we have chosen to do our lives without television. This was a personal conviction for us. When we began our lives together, we didn't want a stranger with a different set of values impacting our marriage or home. We believed we would avoid much temptation toward sexual lust, materialism, wasting time and worldly attitudes. We've had so much more time to pursue the real stuff of life together. We watch sunsets together on the beach rather than on the nature channel. There have been a few downsides to this decision, but the benefits have far outweighed them.

Together for Worship

One of the occupational hazards of ministry is the church becoming the place you minister *instead of* worship as a couple. Avoiding that trap requires you to guard your hearts and ministry practices so that you do *both*. The body of Christ is a gift to us, not just a chore. Each Sunday in our pre-service prayer times, I remind our staff that we are, "worshippers before we are workers. We are sheep before we are shepherds. We are lambs before we are leaders. Do not just give today, receive."

For twenty-six years, Deb and I have been worshipping together at the church we lead. We have been honored to have the same amazing husband-and-wife team, Craig and Mary Durst, leading worship for all those years. The Spirit flows through their ministry. While Deb and I remain the ultimate worship leaders, we also stand with our hands raised together, or receive prayer from our intercessory team, or take communion together kneeling at the front of the church, or receive hugs from the church during the open response time, or weep together as we pray over someone who's hurting. Three services in a row, we expect to meet with God for ourselves and for others.

As leaders, we have to model the worship we hope to see in the marriages of our people. Worship is more caught than taught. I think of Paul's words in 1 Thessalonians 2:8: ". . . Because we loved you so much, we were delighted to share with you not only the gospel of God but our lives as well."

We must be delighted to share not just God's Word, but our lives with the people we're ministering to.

Fighting the Real Enemy

Another essential aspect in the habit of spiritual engagement is the spiritual warfare you wage on behalf of one another. The enemy has drawn a bull's eye on the back of every Christian minister and mate. After describing the demonic powers we battle against (Ephesians 6), Paul pleads with the church of Ephesus, "Pray also for me . . ." (6:19). He understands the reality of demonic resistance and the power we have to confront it.

Understanding that you are your spouse's first line of spiritual intercession dramatically changes your posture. You no longer look at the challenges, conflicts, heartaches, and discouragements as simply circumstantial. They have a spiritual dimension as well. Ecclesiastes 4:12 tells us, "Though one may be overpowered, two can defend themselves. A cord of three strands is not quickly broken." Although this verse isn't written specifically for marriage, we can certainly apply this truth to spiritual warfare. Our response is to rise up with the shield of faith to extinguish the fiery arrows falling on our spouse. Level 5 marriages have become adept at this practice.

As we were writing this chapter, Deb and I prayed for the Lord to speak to hearts. I suddenly had a vivid visual image while I was praying that I want to share because I think it gives us a good picture of how we engage with Jesus and He with us. In the image, Deb and I were sitting in the spinning teacup ride at Disneyland. Our cup had the name "Salvation" painted in red on the side. I could see Jesus at the controls of the ride. The ride started, and we began to circle around, but our teacup didn't spin. We tried to turn the wheel but nothing worked. At first, the ride was fun, but we quickly got bored. The ride stopped, and Deb and I both called out loudly to Jesus, inviting Him to join us in our tea cup. He started the ride again, nimbly jumped into our tea cup and put His hands with ours on the wheel. As we turned the wheel together, the cup began to spin rapidly as we laughed with glee and enjoyed the most incredible ride imaginable. Yes, it still took effort as we partnered with Jesus, but pulling together with Him made all the difference.

Engaging spiritually is a learned habit requiring attention and discipline but it's a practice that produces delight and joy. As you share in spiritual communion in more robust ways, the flow of the Spirit's life into and out of your marriage increases exponentially. As we engage with each other and with the Spirit, we begin to treat each other differently that changes us as individuals, as well as our marriages. We start to honor each other. What does that look like practically? I'm glad you asked.

Assessment: Spiritual Engagement

Using the following scales, rate your marriage 1 to 5 on each of these statements:

1. We consciously include Jesus as our partner in the daily rhythms of our marriage.

1	2	3	4	5
Almost Never	Seldom	Frequently	Usually	Almost Always

2. We are aware of the "one anothers" of Scripture and use them to direct our actions toward each other.

1	2	3	4	5
Almost Never	Seldom	Frequently	Usually	Almost Always

3. We integrate spiritual reality into ordinary moments.

1	2	3	4	5
Almost Never	Seldom	Frequently	Usually	Almost Always

4. We have a basic understanding of the spiritual disciplines and practice them together.

1	2	3	4	5
Almost Never	Seldom	Frequently	Usually	Almost Always

5. We actively pray for each other on a daily basis.

1	2	3	4	5
Almost Never	Seldom	Frequently	Usually	Almost Always

6. We share robust spiritual conversations together.

1	2	3	4	5
Almost Never	Seldom	Frequently	Usually	Almost Always

7. We understand and honor each other's spiritual temperaments.

1	2	3	4	5
Almost Never	Seldom	Frequently	Usually	Almost Always

8. We confess our sins to one another.

1	2	3	4	5
Almost Never	Seldom	Frequently	Usually	Almost Always

9. We actively rid our marriage and lives of sources of temptation in a quest toward holiness.

1	2	3	4	5
Almost Never	Seldom	Frequently	Usually	Almost Always

10. We take spiritual warfare seriously and each day pray for God's shield of faith to cover our spouse.

1	2	3	4	5
Almost Never	Seldom	Frequently	Usually	Almost Always

CHAPTER 5

Habit 3
The Honor You Show

*Be devoted to one another in love.
Honor one another above yourselves.*
(Romans 12:10)

"The beginning of love is the will to let those we love be perfectly themselves, the resolution not to twist them to fit our own image. If in loving them we do not love what they are, but only their potential likeness to ourselves, then we do not love them: we only love the reflection of ourselves we find in them"

—Thomas Merton, No Man Is an Island[1]

Johnny Lingo was a shrewd but honest and well-liked trader in the Polynesian Islands. He came to a particular island to bargain for a wife, as was his custom. His heart was set on a young woman, Mahana, who the other island girls considered ugly and dull. The typical price for a wife was two to four cows depending on her beauty and talents. Knowing Lingo's bargaining prowess and Mahana's undesirability, the islanders began to bet Lingo would offer one cow.

To everyone's shock, Johnny Lingo went to Mahana's father and offered the unheard of price of eight cows. Her father quickly accepted. As the newlyweds left for a long trading trip, the islanders shook their heads at Johnny's foolishness. When the couple finally returned, the islanders could hardly recognize Mahana. She was now a beautiful, bright, and effervescent young woman. The change was so dramatic even her father began to accuse Johnny Lingo of cheating him in the negotiated price!

Johnny knew something every husband and wife should know: When you demonstrate honor to your spouse, you help them blossom into who God created them to be. I remember the first time I heard about *The Legend of Johnny Lingo* and this story. It's such a strong illustration of the third habit we believe is vital for a Level 5 marriage: Honor.

Honor is how you esteem your spouse. It is the internal price you carry around in your head and heart about the worth of the person you married. In short, it's the value you place on them.

But honor is not just the price you "feel" they are worth or could logically "explain" they are worth, it is also the "display" of that value in everyday ways. If Johnny Lingo had paid eight cows but then disregarded Mahana's heart or words on the weekdays, the story would have turned out quite different. This demonstration of value is only honoring if you communicate it in ways your spouse and others understand. It is both a determination and demonstration.

Your spouse is of infinite value and deserving of admiration. Honor is seeing your spouse through God's eyes and then treating them with the kindness and respect that convinces them of their true worth.

Romans 12:10 applies to all believers but especially to your spouse: "Be devoted to one another in love. Honor one another above yourselves." Showing honor is perhaps the most powerful way to express love to your spouse. When you convey honor, you demonstrate your devotion.

Of course, your spouse has their flaws, their personality twitches, their character growth points, their sin struggles, and their bad habits. Seeing our spouse at their worst—when their fatigue opens doors for ugliness; when their stress overwhelms them and they speak unfiltered words; when they leave the toilet seat up despite your pleas—can erode honor.

However, these imperfections never negate your spouse's right to be honored for who they are.

Honor in the Five Levels of Marriage

Level 1 marriages show limited or no honor to their spouse. The wife or husband may make demands to be shown honor, but the requests are ignored. The couple has scant desire to know and value their spouse's gifts. Conversations are a matter of two people talking and no one listening.

Level 2 marriages have a utilitarian approach to showing honor. It has the attitude, "I will honor my wife to the degree it helps me or helps us get along in life. My spouse can do his/her thing as long as it doesn't get in the way of 'my thing.'"

Level 3 marriages have a respect for each other's value. Honor is demonstrated as a matter of duty to God and spouse. It is a 50/50-type of relationship where the spouses meet each other halfway. It's about a *quid pro quo* exchange, something for something. They affirm one another's gifts and encourage them to use them but do little to help them develop them. Ministry discussions center on how their gifts can further the success of their ministries, but personal feelings and dreams are marginalized. They may teach on marriage principles, but they fail to incarnate them.

Level 4 marriages highly value their spouse and have an understanding of his/her uniqueness. They have chosen to demonstrate this value in small and large ways on a daily basis. They take delight in commending their spouse to others apart from themselves and champion their spouse's passions, encouraging them to develop to their fullest potential. Although there is not yet a fully matured ministry camaraderie, they collaborate because they honor one another's input. Conversations are marked by high-quality listening. These couples are often sought out for marriage advice.

Level 5 marriages cherish their spouses without idolizing them. While there is an honesty about their spouse's weaknesses or shortcomings, there is an emphasis on the marvel-ness of their spouse. Gifts, personalities, and passions are thoroughly understood and prized. There is an absolute trust and confidence in the heart of the husband/wife and an exquisite individuality blended with an effective team unity for the sake of the ministry. Level 5 marriages mentor other couples and encourage them to do the same.

Five Reasons for Honor

Our honoring of our spouse flows from five biblical realities:

God's creation. First, we understand them as the one whom the hand of God Himself has crafted. This is where evolutionary thinking so significantly diminishes the value of an individual. Biblical creation causes us to stop and marvel at the handiwork of God in our mate.

God's image. Second, we know our spouse as an image bearer of God. They carry the imprint of God Himself. A part of His nature is resident within them. Our calling is to recognize, admire, and express appreciation for it.

God's salvation. Third, your spouse was esteemed so highly by God that Christ gave Himself for her/him. The Apostle Paul argues from this very rationale in Ephesians: "Husbands, love your wives, just as Christ loved the church and gave himself up for her" (Eph. 5:25).

God's heir. Fourth, our honoring of our spouse arises out of the eternal nature of our relationship. We overrate marriage unless we see it as an earthly, not eternal, institution. For a few short years, we belong to one another as husband and wife. For eternity, we belong to one another as joint-heirs in Christ.

In 1 Peter 3:7 (italics mine), God emphasizes that husbands are commanded to ". . . show her honor as *a fellow heir of the grace of life, so that your prayers will not be hindered.*" Your first approach to your wife is as a sister in Christ or to your husband as a brother in Christ. Honoring our spouse is so essential that it actually diminishes our effectiveness in prayer when we fail to do it.

God's body. Fifth, as members of the body of Christ we each have spiritual gifts and roles within the Church. Although the Church has fallen into worldly thinking by regarding those with public gifts as more honorable than those with more private gifts, Scripture indicates the opposite.

In his first letter to the church in the sexually depraved city of Corinth, Paul writes, "and the parts that we think are less honorable we treat with special honor . . . But God has put the body together, giving greater honor to the parts that lacked it, so that there should be no division in the body, but that its parts should have equal concern for each other" (1 Cor. 12:23-25).

When we truly honor our spouse's gifts and roles within the church, we carry out the intention of Christ for His body. We reject the worldly assessment of those who assign status based on notoriety.

My Broken Journey

I had to learn this the hard way. For many years in our marriage, I believed my gifts were the important ones and Deb's spiritual gifts were to help me be more effective—to help me shine. I wrongly reasoned her path to being honored was through helping me be more honored by the church and the world. If she lost her life for my sake, she would find it.

Unfortunately for the first eleven years of our marriage, we ministered under some abusive spiritual teaching that reinforced this bogus thinking. I failed to honor Deb for who she was and the gifts God had given her. I was frustrated with her because she failed to "honor" me by being insufficiently supportive of my calling and gifts. Meanwhile, Deb was shrinking inside, diminished by my arrogance. Her insecurity in her own value, apart from me, was strangling her spiritual life and inhibiting her ministry effectiveness.

Whenever I read Proverbs 31 about the virtuous wife, I am impressed by how strong, secure, and gifted this noble woman is. She knows her own gifts and strengths and uses them to build up and bless her family. She is buying property, starting businesses, and making investments on her own, with no mention of her husband's involvement. She is confident but not independent. Her husband has his gifts and work, and she has hers. Together they are an influential team.

The first descriptive statement about her is, "Her husband has full confidence in her" (31:11). This guy doesn't hold his wife back. Instead, he says, "Go for it, honey! You can do this!" Her husband calls her "blessed" (31:28) and has a habit of praising her. Proverbs 31 ends with the command to "honor her" for who she is and what she has done (31:31).

In mine and Deb's case, I was receiving more and more applause. But unlike the Proverbs 31 woman, Deb's gifts were being ignored by me, by others, and by Deb herself. She was losing the courage to be who God made her to be and do what she was capable of doing.

As we left our toxic church, I slowly awakened to my misguided approach to our marriage. I encouraged Deb to go back for her Master's degree in marriage and family therapy. I began to see how my lack of honoring Deb had contributed to her shortage of confidence to reach her full potential. I began to take steps to more fully grasp who Deb was, her gifts and personality. As a result, her security and influence started to grow. We would have more challenges and setbacks, but now we were headed in the right direction.

Discovering Your Spouse

Many marriages never move to higher levels of honoring because they fail to delve deeply into who their spouse really is. We assume we know one another well. After all, we live together daily. We see each other at our worst. It is that daily-ness, however, that can become the clouds obscuring the gold in our spouse. Because we see them in their frustration, exhaustion, anger, confusion, and distraction, we lose sight of their amazing potential.

Do you know your spouse's strengths? Our marriage took a major leap forward when we took the StrengthsFinder test. We invested the time and money to really learn each other's strengths, as well as the dark sides of those strengths. The assessment gave us words to use to describe each other's personalities. Attributes that had frustrated us about each other became points of celebration as we understood how they could be employed to build our family and ministry.

For example, Deb has the Arranger strength. I have the Positivity strength. She wants to plan it all out. I think it will just all work out great. If I honor her strength, we are golden. If I honor only my strength, I can get us into trouble quickly. If Deb discounts my strength, she can easily see all the reasons something will not work and will pull back. But if she gleans from my strength, she can find logic to move forward.

Deb and I took other evaluations as well. The DISC test, the Myers-Briggs test, vocational tests, skills tests, leadership styles tests, Love Languages, spiritual gifts tests—all have contributed to our understanding of one another. We began to genuinely value our differences.

Celebrating Differences

One of the most dishonoring actions I had taken in our relationship was to try to make Deb more like me. If she could just "feel," "reason," "respond," and "act" like I did, then we could achieve so much more with much less tension. Not only was I marginalizing her and desecrating the greatness God has instilled in her, I was missing what we could gain from her contributions. It was like we were in a race, but I had chosen to carry her because I didn't think she could run it on her own. I wasn't helping her, and I was hurting myself.

As we began to seek the insights of others, we frequently asked those closest to us, "What gifts and talents do you see in each of us?" When you're so close to someone, you can lose perspective. The feedback of others helped us gain objectivity. The result was we valued one another more. I have stood back in amazement as Deb has blossomed into the fullness of her calling and ministry. I understand I'm biased, but she is now the most Proverbs 31 woman I have ever met.

Honoring one another is knowing the correct and detailed answers to questions like:

What makes my spouse's heart sing?
What delights him/her?
What disturbs him/her?
What comes naturally to my spouse?
What restores him/her?
What depletes him/her?
What increases his/her courage?
What defeats him/her?
What is his/her idea of a "good time"?
What are his/her fears?
What keeps him/her up at night?
What are his/her dreams?

Since 1981, our best friends have been Dwight and Shelley Pauls. They are bivocational ministry gurus. Dwight owns a successful company, and Shelley is in management at Alaska Airlines. Together, they accomplish more for the gospel than most full-time pastoral couples we know. Shelley's passions and gifts revolve around mobilizing God's people to serve the hurting and poor. She has the strength of Arranger and the gift of Leadership. Dwight has a servant's heart, a brilliant mind and skillful hands capable of doing anything. He has the gift of Helping. Their honor for each other has released their gifts individually, and they are a formidable team as they integrate their strengths. Recently, they have been mobilizing dozens of churches to work together to do city-transforming service events. They have also personally organized and led dozens of mission trips. Hundreds of people in the United States and around the world have been impacted by the Pauls' marriage. They honor their differences while teaming together for the gospel.

The Honor of Listening

The Book of James gives us one of the most helpful pieces of marriage advice, which is also one of the highest forms of honor: "My dear brothers and sisters, take note of this: Everyone should be quick to listen, slow to speak and slow to become angry" (James 1:19). Deep listening is a display of high honor. Every person wants to be heard and understood. Giving your attention and time to really help your spouse feel heard communicates great value.

Over the last twenty-five years, we have needed to hire many pastors to help us serve our church, which sends out leaders and church plants. One of the traits we always look for is, "How well does this candidate listen to their spouse?" We watch their body language as their spouse talks. Is the listening spouse truly attentive? Are they affirming? Are they quick to correct a missed or incorrect detail? Are they interrupting? Does the spouse seem free to share his/her own opinion, or does he/

she have to offer the same answer as the spouse? The answers to these questions can take you behind the doors of a marriage to uncover how much honor is really happening in these homes.

Honor in the Small Places

To build a Level 5 marriage, your honoring of one another must mature so that it permeates the entire relationship. You seek to understand the small ways you can daily demonstrate her/his value to you. Small acts of kindness and thoughtfulness display honor. The Holy Spirit is not just interested in transforming the major events of honor. The Spirit always wants to flow into the cracks and crevices of our relationship. The seemingly mundane minutiae is the place God wants to get His fingers deep into the clay of our lives.

In the spirit of transparency, I had a bad habit of dropping my clothes on the bedroom floor at night and running off the next morning. I knew this bothered Deb, but in reality I felt, *Hey, I'm the busier one in this family. It's not that big a deal. Surely you can pick up my clothes to help me out a little.* A couple of years ago, Deb and I had one of our "DTRs" (Discussing the Relationship) talks. She let me know I was dishonoring her by my refusal to care for my own clothes. It was no small thing to her. Once I understood it as a matter of honor, rather than preference, I was motivated to change. Now I think I'm about ninety percent healed; Deb would say, seventy-five.

Most spouses we've seen don't understand how influential their words about their spouse are, even when their husband/wife is absent. We honor our husbands/wives with our words, especially as we talk to others about them. While bragging on your spouse can sometimes be self-serving, we should always be quick to champion them in conversations, especially if they're with us. My ministry is more public so I'm often the recipient of compliments, which makes it especially important for me to help others understand what a phenomenal minister Deb is.

Honoring Both Callings

Level 5 marriages understand how to honor each other's unique calling while working together in God's calling as a couple. This dynamic isn't always easily discerned, but it can be powerful when we pursue it. When one spouse's calling is prioritized to the detriment of the other partner's calling, both end up losing. Certainly, there are times when one mate's callings will drive the decision (such as when to move to take a different job). In those moments, we have to think and pray long and hard about how to make the change a win/win for both spouse's callings.

We've experienced this firsthand. I was offered the pastorate of an affluent megachurch three times the size of our church. The call appealed to me. Deb, however, would have had to leave her successful ministry and try to re-create it in the new place. She was willing to honor my calling if I was convinced God was in it. I considered seriously the impact upon Deb's current ministry. As we prayed and weighed the decision, it became apparent to us both that changing locations was more a "career move" than a "God-call." We declined, and both our ministries seemed to take a significant step forward.

In Level 5 marriages, the primary ministry of both partners has become, "making disciples who make disciples." Although many other ministry roles may be carried out, the main thing is this form of ministry multiplication. Regardless of gifting or personality strengths, husbands and wives challenge each other to this biblical priority. Honoring one another in this regard means to help one another carry out this mandate.

The Navigators ministry is famed for its emphasis on disciple making, which sprang not just from the teaching of their founder, Dawson Trotman, but from the living example of Dawson and his wife, Lila Mae. Although their gifts and personalities were quite different, the couple was passionate about making disciples. Their home was continually filled with young women that Lila Mae was discipling and young men that Dawson was training. What started as a small spark spread person by person to eventually become The Navigators, a worldwide partnership that today has more than 4,000 staff ministering in 110 countries. When Dawson drowned at age fifty, Lila kept right on making disciples. She shaped the lives of many Navigator women, and Dawson often said that without her and her willingness to open her home, there would never have been a Navigators ministry. Dawson's honoring of his wife helped lead to a worldwide impact.[2]

God has gospel intentions for your spouse and your marriage. As you make a habit of honoring your spouse, the treasure He has invested in him/her is distributed to an impoverished world. With honor comes the important habit of inspiring passion in each other. Read on as we look at another game changer for our marriage.

Assessment: Showing Honor

Using the following scale, rate your marriage 1 to 5 on each of these statements:

1. We view each other as "made in the image of God" and see part of God's nature through one another.

1	2	3	4	5
Almost Never	Seldom	Frequently	Usually	Almost Always

2. We view each other as sister or brother first, then as wife or husband.

1	2	3	4	5
Almost Never	Seldom	Frequently	Usually	Almost Always

3. We understand and value one another's strengths and talents.

1	2	3	4	5
Almost Never	Seldom	Frequently	Usually	Almost Always

4. We understand and value one another's spiritual gifts.

1	2	3	4	5
Almost Never	Seldom	Frequently	Usually	Almost Always

5. We speak well of one another in each other's absence.

1	2	3	4	5
Almost Never	Seldom	Frequently	Usually	Almost Always

6. We practice listening deeply to one another.

1	2	3	4	5
Almost Never	Seldom	Frequently	Usually	Almost Always

7. We address habits our spouse finds dishonoring.

1	2	3	4	5
Almost Never	Seldom	Frequently	Usually	Almost Always

8. We seek to open doors of opportunity for our spouse's passions.

1	2	3	4	5
Almost Never	Seldom	Frequently	Usually	Almost Always

9. We honor each other's callings and seek to integrate them.

1	2	3	4	5
Almost Never	Seldom	Frequently	Usually	Almost Always

10. We readily recognize and celebrate each other's wins.

1	2	3	4	5
Almost Never	Seldom	Frequently	Usually	Almost Always

CHAPTER 6

Habit 4
The Passion You Inspire

"And let us consider how we may spur one another on toward love and good deeds."
(Hebrews 10:24)

"The best love is the kind that awakens the soul and makes us reach for more, that plants a fire in our hearts and brings peace to our minds."
Nicholas Sparks, *The Notebook*[1]

One of the only times I have ever heard Deb swear was when I attempted to be a motivational voice. In 1977, she was selected as a college campus student leader at Azusa Pacific College. She would soon join twenty other student leaders for a seven-day wilderness experience in the Sierra Nevada mountains. The time together would culminate with an eight-mile run/walk each participant had to finish.

It was the same summer we spent with my family in Kansas (the summer I proposed), and Deb asked me to be her trainer/coach to help her finish the upcoming eight-mile run. Running ahead of her in the ninety-five-degree Kansas heat, loudly exhorting her to go faster, I thought I was doing a great job of inspiring passion in my new fiancée.

"You're dogging it," I yelled in my best coaching voice. "You're trudging, not running! You're not trying! You'll never finish the race, training like this!"

At that point, Deb let me know she was passionate "at" me, not "about" me. It was not a good moment in our engagement story.

We've spent the next forty years learning how to inspire passion in one another. Deb has become an expert at it, and I'm advancing. One of our convictions: *Passion is essential and available to live the abundant life God created us for.*

The Passion Priority

If there's one thing I've learned as both a husband, father, and pastor it's that God doesn't give commands we can't keep if we rely on the help of His Spirit to follow them. One such command comes from Romans 12:11: "Never be lacking in zeal, but keep your spiritual fervor, serving the Lord." God directs us to keep our zeal and fervor levels high. Then He points our passion toward serving His mission.

We agree with what the late Steve Jobs said in his commencement address to Stanford University: "The only way to do great work is to love what you do."[2] The level of our passions will be a key factor in our effectiveness in marriage and ministry.

Before we go any further, we want to be really clear about what passion isn't and what it is. Passion is not a mystical feeling coming and going based on our whims or circumstances. Passion or zeal is something we control (Rom. 12:11). It is an attitude we choose, a decision to earnestly care about valuable things, and a mindset of enthusiasm about life and all good gifts from God.

Passion is the zest of living. Whether we point our passion toward God, our spouse, our children, our ministry, or life itself, passion is the force that empowers us to keep going when it's hard; to endure pain for a worthwhile goal; to enjoy the journey; and to celebrate small victories.

Passion is what makes her/his face exciting to wake up to forty years after you first met. It's what keeps you on your knees with your Bible on your bed, anticipating the voice of his Spirit. Passion is the factor causing you to anticipate Sunday's service and what God might break forth to accomplish there. It is the element getting you out of a warm bed to watch a glorious sunrise on a cold morning.

Passion in the Five Levels of Marriage

Level 1 marriages have no passion except perhaps outbursts of anger toward one another.

Level 2 marriages survive mostly on memories of passion with occasional tastes of what used to be.

Level 3 marriages exist amid a low level of passion and major in seeking to create moments of extreme—what we would call "Hollywood" passion that only exists on a stage or movie set.

Level 4 marriages have moved to a mutual effort to stoke passion in one another for life and ministry.

Level 5 marriages have mature passion where each spouse understands and practices motivating the other toward spiritual zeal for the sake of the Kingdom. They share a three-pronged passion for each other, for life and for ministry.

The Mandate to Motivate

One of the great marriage verses of the Bible often isn't recognized that way. But for us, Hebrews 10:24 has marriage written all over it: "And let us consider how we may spur one another on toward love and good deeds." The New American Standard translation says, "and let us consider how to stimulate one another to love and good deeds," (NAS) while the New Living Translation reads, "Let us think of ways to motivate one another to acts of love and good works" (NLT). If this scripture applies to our brothers and sisters in Christ, then surely it's even more applicable to our spouse.

The idea is clear: We should give careful and creative attention to motivating our spouses forward toward more love and acts of goodness. God points out that we are His tools to help inspire one another. Our goals of more love and more good ministry are worthy and attainable dreams. We need to motivate and be motivated by our husband/wife.

Motivational Failures: Five Factors

In hindsight, I realize my efforts to motivate Deb to run harder in the Kansas heat were inept due to five factors. Deb and I see these same failures plaguing marriages.

I was passionate about something she wasn't. Deb wanted to be able to finish the race. I wanted her to be able to win. Her dream was different than mine. You infuse passion when you listen well enough to understand the dream in your spouse's heart and then join in.

I was running ahead of her, not beside her. I thought if I ran a little faster than she did, it would inspire her. Instead, my actions discouraged her and made her feel like she couldn't measure up. We pass on passion when we're really with our spouse in the place they are and walking beside them to a place they want to go. We can't stress that enough.

I was speaking my motivational language, not hers. My football coach yelled tough statements at us, and our team rose to accept the challenge. My statements of loving encouragement—not condemnation—motivate Deb. We impart passion when we know what inspires our spouse and then do more of it.

I confused "trying harder" with "trying smarter." In my small mind, the answer was always just "try harder." I never considered strategies that may have helped her improve more quickly. Passion increases when you're taking the most effective routes toward your dreams. Detours kill passion.

I used fear of failure to try to push her forward. Fear can be a great motivator but not if it leads to unbelief. Not believing you can move forward, go faster, do better, or finish what you start will kill passion. I was speaking fear instead of faith to Deb.

Shocker! Deb fired me as her coach. She continued with the encouragement of others to devotedly train throughout the summer. When the final race came, she finished first among the women and third overall. Her passion and practice carried her to the finish line.

The Four Directions of Passion

As we worked through this topic and chapter together, Deb and I began to identify four specific directions of passion that we believe and have seen firsthand as integral to becoming a Level 5 marriage:

A passion for God: Passion is one of the most accurate English words to summarize Jesus' great command. He said the most important act of every human is to be passionate for God. The word "all" is repeated four times in Mark 12:30 (italics mine): "Love the Lord your God with *all* your heart and with *all* your soul and with *all* your mind and with *all* your strength.'" In that one verse, Jesus rules out a ho-hum approach to spiritual life. An all-powerful, all-knowing, all-present, all-compassionate God is worthy of an all-consuming love.

Level 5 marriages understand this passionate pursuit as the priority of their lives. Their first commitment is to help one another to live out God's first command—understanding that both pursuing and keeping that commitment produces the most fulfilling and fruitful life possible. They look for creative ways to encourage each other toward greater passion in their personal knowledge and love of Jesus.

Ministry can diminish or even replace our love for God. We can fall in love with the work of the Lord instead of the Lord of the work. The difference is subtle, especially at first, but the impact is profound. Deb and I often question each other to help us think through where the source of our passion lies. Is it based on who God *is* or what He is *doing*?

It's wonderful to get excited about what God is doing in our lives and churches, but when it comes down to it, our passion should be rooted in our relationship with Him—who He is as our Creator and Savior. We want to help each other be like Paul who at the end of his ministry still fervently cried out, "I want to know Christ . . . and become like him" (Phil. 3:10).

A passion for ministry: Second to a passion for God is a passion for ministry that inspires passion in one another for the ministry call upon our lives. As leaders, we have a responsibility to stoke the fire. Some leaders I've known act like ministry passion is either automatic or optional. Neither is true.

In His instructions to the priests in the Old Testament, God gives us a word picture for our New Testament ministries: "The fire on the altar must be kept burning; it must not go out. Every morning the priest is to add firewood . . ." (Lev. 6:12). Then in the New Testament, Paul spoke to his son in the faith about Timothy's passion for ministry. He says to him, ". . . I remind you to fan into flame the gift of God, which is in you through the laying on of my hands" (2 Tim. 1:6). In essence,

Paul told Timothy, his son in the faith, "Just because you have a gift doesn't necessarily mean you're passionate about it. Do what it takes to turn up the heat!" Our spouse can be one of God's primary "fans" to stir up our ministry flame.

Two truths Deb is excellent to remind me about are the individuality and the eternal nature of our work. When you understand the value that God places on the life of one person, seeing just one person move toward God can inspire you. Small spiritual victories in someone's life really matter. And when you begin to comprehend the seriousness and privilege of leveraging your brief life toward "eternal impact" on others, it propels you.

Deb and I also confront each other when comparison whispers in our ears. Nothing quenches passion like comparison. Scrolling through Facebook and seeing your neighboring pastor's church packed when yours was half-full on Sunday can drain you. Going to ministry conferences to hear the star pastors tell you what they did and that if you just do it their way, it will work for you too, can sap your strength. Staring at the impact of someone else's ministry takes our eyes off God and the lane He has assigned to us. Competition is for athletics, not ministry. We're much healthier when our only desire is to improve our personal best and build unity. Comparison will quickly deplete our ministry passion.

Unless we learn the art of reframing, we cannot stay resilient and passionate in ministry. Practicing God's ministry with broken people will knock us down time and again. Often, our goals will be thwarted and we'll face disappointment. When you take your disappointment or setback and see it differently, you reframe it. Resiliency is essential in ministry, and reframing what can be difficult realities is a key to resiliency. When something negative happens, we tend to tighten the frame, highlighting the pain we're feeling. We focus on the setback and lose the bigger picture.

Another way to say it is that reframing puts the frame around the whole picture of God's work. We don't deny the pain but instead place it in its true context: God is still at work. God is good. God's scorecard is different than the world's. When we put the setback in an eternal frame, the disappointment diminishes in magnitude. Deb and I constantly help each other reframe our perspective to create resiliency and renew a passion.

A passion for life: Third on the passion list is the vital importance of inspiring a passion for life in one another. Deb and I often remind ourselves of two of our favorite quotes:

- "Many people die at age 25 but aren't buried until they're 75" (Benjamin Franklin).
- The other is from one of our favorite movies, *Dead Poets Society*. John Keating, played by Robin Williams, is directing his students to look at the class picture from previous decades and asks the class of young men, "Did they wait until it was too late to make their lives even one iota of what they were capable? Because, you see gentleman, these boys are now fertilizing daffodils. But if you listen real close, you can hear them whisper their legacy to you . . . *Carpe* . . . hear it? *Carpe, carpe diem*, seize the day boys, make your lives extraordinary!"[3]

Our marriages can suck the life out of us or infuse us with extraordinary energy to *carpe diem*—to live all the way to the finish line. When Deb and I made our marriage vows, we determined our mission would be to help each other "be fully alive!" Yes, there would be dirty dishes, dirty diapers, and dirty floors. But we purposed to refuse to let the daily duties of living squeeze the adventure of living out of our lives. We will be "fertilizing daffodils" soon enough, but between here and there we'll shake each other awake to life.

One of my favorite cards I've received from Deb had the simple words: "I like me best when I'm with you." The feeling is mutual. We make it a point to wake each other up, refusing to let each other sleepwalk. I think of the often-quoted Proverb: "As iron sharpens iron, so one person sharpens another" (Prov. 27:17). The Level 5 marriage is dedicated to the quest of daily sharpening, producing a growing alertness and aliveness to this amazing journey called life.

We sharpen each other when we point out beauty to one another. Deb's really good at this. She'll often say, "Look at this flower, listen to this song, see that bird, notice her smile, smell the air today, taste this recipe, feel this fabric." She motivates me to be fully present in the moment, to experience God in His small, daily gifts to us.

One of our college professors taught us, "The person who is content with little has a continual feast." I love that. We don't heighten our passion by increasing our income, possessions, or congregation size, but by adjusting our attitude and focus. This is why God tells us ". . . the cheerful heart has a continual feast" (Prov. 15:15). If we live dreaming of that island called "Someday," we'll miss what God is doing today, right here, right now.

An important sidebar: Be aware of clinical depression. It's a reality for many and just, "deciding to be passionate" or, "believing your spouse can be the answer to your depression" are unrealistic and unhealthy. If you or your spouse have been diagnosed as clinically depressed or you suspect it, we strongly encourage you to get professional help.

A passion for each other: The fourth and final dimension of passion in a Level 5 marriage focuses on your spouse. Do you remember what it felt like to be so "in love" you thought of him or her multiple times in one hour? I have an entry in my diary (before we called them journals) from when I met Deb, and all it says is "WOW!" in all caps filling the page. It was pure emotion. After nearly forty years of marriage, there is still a "wow!," but it's filled with thousands of pieces of data, interactions and reflections. It is the difference in the passion of puppy love and that of seasoned love.

Level 5 marriages inspire a passion we call "romance in real time." Hollywood wants to sell us a version of passion built around sexuality and unrealistic moments. But we have a God who's all about truth. He created us for a passion inclusive of our daily routines and our physical actualities.

When God describes His idea of passion in a marriage over the long haul, it looks like Proverbs 5:18-19: "May your fountain be blessed, and may you rejoice in the wife of your youth. A loving doe, a graceful deer—may her breasts satisfy you always, may you ever be intoxicated with her love." This blessing from Solomon to his son is a robust articulation of physical, sexual, and emotional connection for a lifetime.

At the same time, these verses describe how you feel when the kids are sick, the car is in the shop, the washing machine just broke, and the church board meeting is tonight. How does "romance" break into real-time moments like this? Although you might wisely share a kiss of empathy in the middle of the chaos, romance is "on hold." But "on hold" does not mean "ignored" or "forgotten." If you allow those real-life moments to fill up your calendar without prioritizing time to do what you did when you were first in love, passion will soon go flat.

In a marriage, passion is really three languages: his, hers, and ours. Becoming fluent in all three languages is helpful and delightful. In his classic work, *The 5 Love Languages*, author Gary Chapman defines five basic languages: physical touch, quality time, acts of service, gifts, and words of affirmation. My love language is "physical touch"; Deb's is "acts of service." If Deb comes home to find me on my knees scrubbing the kitchen floor, she starts to feel the love glow. The same is true if I'm in my chair doing sermon prep, and she comes up and runs her fingers through my hair while kissing me on the cheek.

But there's also "our" love language—understanding what we do together to create a mood that fosters passion and intimacy. This isn't just the standard bubble baths, candles, chocolates and perfumes (though these can definitely be inspirational). Deb and I have learned to identify and pursue the settings, conversations, preludes, atmospheres, and spaces where we're both most likely to "feel the love tonight."

True Intimacy

Understanding intimacy is a prerequisite for inspiring passion in your marriage. When God told us that, "two shall become one," He was talking about much more than sexual intimacy. God made us with a longing for intimacy. The Trinity itself is the ultimate example, understanding "the three are one." Intimacy involves a closeness, a being fully known by another even as you know them fully. It is a sharing of life, of heart, of personality, of hopes, dreams, fears, joys . . . and yes, as husband and wife, a physical sharing in sexuality.

I once heard someone say that we can understand intimacy's true meaning by sounding out the word: "in-to-me-see." It is the blending of our lives so that you can "see into" who your spouse really is and he/she can "see into" you. Intimacy is multi-dimensional.

We suggest pursuing ten types of intimacy:

1. Emotional intimacy: a deep sharing of significant feelings.
2. Intellectual intimacy: sharing the world of thoughts, ideas, and opinions.
3. Work intimacy: sharing chores around the home, working together to make a home.
4. Creative intimacy: sharing in acts of creating (cooking, building, growing, painting, writing).

5. Recreational intimacy: sharing in hobbies, pleasures, diversions, and travel.
6. Spiritual intimacy: sharing in prayer, Scripture, and spiritual gifts.
7. Financial intimacy: openly sharing financial realities and dreams.
8. Aesthetic intimacy: sharing experiences of beauty (nature, music, art, etc.).
9. Physical intimacy: sharing non-sexual displays of affection.
10. Sexual intimacy: sharing yourselves fully with each other in acts of sexual pleasure.

Level 5 marriages give attention to maturing in all ten forms of intimacy. The payoff is a passion that grows all the way to death. Our great joy is in becoming adept at inspiring passion in one another.

Fencing Off Our Passion

A final aspect of passion is the necessity of building clear boundaries, like a fence, around our relationship with God and each other. Boundary markers delineate where your property stops and starts. God cares about boundaries. He even talks about them specifically: "Cursed is anyone who moves their neighbor's boundary stone. Then all the people shall say, 'Amen!'" (Deut. 27:17).

Boundaries in our lives communicate, "This is my marriage property, my ministry property and my personal property. You cannot come through this fence unless I say so." If you're in any form of ministry, I don't have to tell you that ministry is filled with boundary busters—people who barge in and start to take over with their latest crisis. If we don't set, guard, and enforce clear boundaries, people and circumstances will drain our zeal. And when it happens, the only one to blame is yourself for not building those fences.

Over the years, Deb and I have learned to protect our time together. For example, we have insisted on a date night for all of our married lives. When people want to cross our boundary with their latest marriage emergency, we have learned to say, "This emergency didn't happen overnight, and it won't steal our date night tonight. We can see you tomorrow or later this week." (The "boundaries" concept has been clearly written about by John Townsend and Henry Cloud. Their book, *Boundaries in Marriage*, is a wonderful guide to creating healthy boundaries. Also, Brian and Amy Bloye talk about setting boundaries in their excellent book, *It's Personal*.)

If we fail to set boundaries to protect our personal time, our marriage time, our family time, our recreational time, etc., then people, ministry projects, board expectations, (the list goes on and on) will run all over our property and destroy our passion in the process.

A Day of Passion

Nine years following my coaching failure with Deb's training in the Kansas heat, I fulfilled a big dream and ran across the finish line of the Seattle Marathon. Leading up to it, I spent six months training hard. When the day finally arrived, Deb drove the course with a few friends to cheer me on. Every few miles, they would see me and shout encouragement.

I was running strong and could feel my dream coming true . . . until mile twenty-three. I suddenly felt a sharp pain in my foot (I discovered later it was a stress fracture). At that moment, Deb pulled the car near me; she could tell I was in pain. Someone in the car shouted, "It's okay to quit. You've run enough. Don't hurt yourself!" But Deb, seeing the determination in my eyes, handed over the steering wheel to a friend, jumped out of the car in her street shoes and started running alongside me. For the next three miles she ran with me, earnestly encouraging me, "You can do it, Honey. Don't stop! You are strong! I am with you!" Now she was the one inspiring me to run. She did it the right way.

Her words and commitment inspired an incredible passion in me. We finished together.

Marriage and ministry are marathons not sprints. It will be painful at times. Quitting or slowing down will be easy and might even seem justified at times. But we're confident in saying that building a marriage with a habit of inspiring passion for God, for ministry, for life and for each other will motivate you to run all the way to the finish line.

Assessment: Inspiring Passion

Using the following scales for each question, rate your marriage 1 to 5 on each of these statements:

1. We believe being passionate about God and His Kingdom is an essential command to be integrated into our marriage.

1	2	3	4	5
Not true at all	Somewhat True	Basically True	True	Very True

2. We understand each other's motivational language and actively seek to speak it.

1	2	3	4	5
Not true at all	Somewhat True	Basically True	True	Very True

3. We inspire each other by "running alongside" one another. We feel "with" each other.

1	2	3	4	5
Not true at all	Somewhat True	Basically True	True	Very True

4. We are more passionate about Jesus than we are about ministry for Jesus.

1	2	3	4	5
Not true at all	Somewhat True	Basically True	True	Very True

5. We "seize the day" by making living a daily adventure.

1	2	3	4	5
Not true at all	Somewhat True	Basically True	True	Very True

6. We bring out the best in each other.

1	2	3	4	5
Not true at all	Somewhat True	Basically True	True	Very True

7. Our sexual intimacy is satisfying to both of us.

1	2	3	4	5
Not true at all	Somewhat True	Basically True	True	Very True

8. We understand the different dimensions of intimacy and are actively pursuing them.

1	2	3	4	5
Not true at all	Somewhat True	Basically True	True	Very True

9. We help each other "reframe" disappointing situations.

1	2	3	4	5
Not true at all	Somewhat True	Basically True	True	Very True

10. We "fire each other up" for the ministries we pursue and engage.

1	2	3	4	5
Not true at all	Somewhat True	Basically True	True	Very True

CHAPTER 7

Habit 5
Vision Alignment

*Can two people walk together without
agreeing on the direction?*
Amos 3:3 (NLT)

*If you want to go fast, go alone.
If you want to go far, go together.*
—African Proverb

*Love does not consist of gazing at each other, but in
looking outward together in the same direction.*
– Antoine de Saint-Exupéry

Deb and I were dancing cheek-to-cheek to Chris Botti's, "Italia" on the veranda of our secluded Tuscany villa—one of our top ten most romantic moments, for sure.

But we almost missed that moment.

A few hours earlier, we were raising our voices in a heated discussion (some would label it an argument) as each of us hurled blame in the other person's direction. Our church had given us a three-month sabbatical, and through the kindness of some friends, we got the opportunity to spend some of it in the hills of Chianti, Italy, writing this book. Great plan, except it involved renting a car and navigating some busy, then-remote parts of Italy. With confidence, we thought,

Hey, we're a team. Deb navigates with the help of Google maps, and Larry drives. What could go wrong? Plenty.

When you don't know where you're going, the road ahead can lead to nowhere.

When you're listening to conflicting voices, the drive can be confusing and full of conflict. In our case, we had the name of the area but not the address of the villa. When we stopped multiple times to ask for directions, we got conflicting advice each time. At times, we had three divergent voices speaking urgently in the car: Deb's, mine and the Google girl.

We had agreed that since Deb was looking at the map, she would call out directions, and I would follow them. This approach worked fairly well until I disagreed with Deb on a major turn (actually more than one turn). One particular wrong turn led to a lengthy delay and a "pull over, cool off" time (or what I would call "putting me in a time-out").

The answers we needed finally came when we arrived to the general area of where we were staying. Then we reached the owner of the villa to get the actual address. Once we knew our destination and agreed on how to get there, we worked efficiently as a team.

Our Vision Fail

Our Italian driving adventure became a lesson in aligning our vision in life and ministry. On that tension-filled journey:

1. We lacked clarity about where we were heading.
   (We need to know where we're trying to go in marriage and ministry.)
2. Our communication about the journey broke down.
   (We can't do our share of the vision if we don't actually share about the vision.)

3. I was making decisions without consulting the map.
   (Our visions and decisions are directed by the authority of the Word.)
4. We were in a hurry to arrive and missed the scenery on the way.
   (The beauty is in the journey, not just the destination . . . laugh along the way.)
5. When we worked together, we arrived.
   (Teamwork makes the dream work. A bit trite, but true.)
6. The destination was amazing . . . beyond our dreams.
   (Jesus promised that journeying with Him would mean experiencing far beyond what we could imagine.)

Aligning our vision can take us farther than we imagined and make the trip there more joy than burden. First, however, we must understand vision and how it applies in our marriage.

The Anatomy of Vision

Level 5 Marriages have aligned their individual, marriage and ministry visions. We can define "vision" in multiple ways, but the essential characteristics of vision include:

1. Visual – Vision is a mental picture, an imagined scenario, a description you can talk and write about.
2. Desirable – Vision is something preferable, beyond your current reality, a desire, dream or goal.
3. Future – Vision has a time element to it. It can be your vision for this week, this year, this decade, this life, or even for eternity.
4. Actionable – Vision is different from wishing or dreaming. We can take pragmatic steps toward vision and vision alignment.
5. Surrendered – Vision comes out of a desire to follow God's call; we hold it loosely in submission to His direction.
6. Shared – Vision in a marriage is never just individual. Since you're one with your spouse, you integrate your vision with hers/his.

The sad reality is that most married couples never invest in discovering and clarifying their vision. Consequently, they end up in a life-long situation similar to the short-term one we created in Italy. In a moment of extreme ambiguity over our destination, we arrived at a rather large round-about. We disagreed which round-about exit was correct, and as a result we simply drove in circles as we argued. Many marriages have much discussion and motion. But without a clear vision, the energy we use results in circles instead of progress.

Receiving, clarifying and aligning vision is a lifelong process but begins and advances with a commitment to a common destination. It's a devotion to assist one another in becoming and doing all he/she can for the Kingdom.

Vision Alignment in the Five Levels of Marriage

Level 1: In the Consumer marriage, each person has a vision for himself/herself only. Each may use his/her spouse to reach their own goals without regard for their spouse's own call.

Level 2: Convenient marriages have no real vision except making life easier and sustainable. Keeping up the status quo for the sake of the marriage, the kids, and the church is as far-reaching as their vision goes.

Level 3: Committed marriages have a vision for success, results, and goal accomplishment. Usually, however, these visions are not win/win for both spouses but rather for their individual ministry and reputation.

Level 4: Collaborative marriages have a vision for working together for the good of one another *and* the ministry. They want to see each other make a high impact using their individual gifts. They have a desire to reproduce their marriage quality and ministry in others.

Level 5: Communion marriages have a vision for sharing all they are for the sake of one another and ministry impact. They envision empowering each other toward a fullness of joy and fruitfulness. Their goals flow out of deeply shared values. They desire to multiply their faith, mission, and marriages into the lives of individuals and couples who will do the same for others. They are not interested in being heroes but in making heroes.

Vision Problems

When tires are out of alignment on a car, they affect the car's speed, waste fuel, cause a rougher ride, wear out the tires faster, and create other problems. When the alignment is off, the trip is shaky. The same is true for vision alignment in a marriage. Alignment allows the marriage to accomplish Kingdom mission with greater speed and effectiveness. It decreases wasted energies. Just like car tires, our marriages need regular vision alignments. Sometimes we need to take our marriages to a professional for help in aligning them.

Eleven years in, Deb and I hit a big speed bump that knocked our marriage far out of alignment. The megachurch we were youth pastors at had just imploded (due to the pastor's carnality), destroying our jobs, our paycheck, our place of worship, and many of our friendships. Even though we were both hurting, I had dogmatic ideas about where we were headed next. Deb disagreed. I powered up. Deb pulled back her heart. She felt we needed help to realign our marriage. I did not. As usual, she was the wiser one. She finally convinced me, and we sought out some professional help, which helped us realign our marriage and move forward on God's road for us.

Deb and I are often shocked by how much couples will spend on entertainment, sports, dinners out, and vacations and how little they'll invest in their marriage. Marriage books, seminars, and especially marriage counseling are often the highest-return investment you can make in life. When Deb was practicing as a professional therapist, she counseled hundreds of couples and not one ended up saying, "Well, we blew that money."

Individual Vision Alignment

As an individual, you need vision. Where are you taking your life? Do you have values you want to turn into vision? Do you have goals? Do you have dreams (not fantasies) you're praying toward?

In a marriage. you can have the powerful help of a dream partner. Your spouse can be the one who helps birth your dreams. Through prayer, encouragement, questions, and cheering, your spouse can help you see and seize your future.

Some of the saddest marriages we see are when one spouse has dreams, and the other spouse has none. Often, this is because the dominating spouse has been a dream crusher. Rather than nurturing their mate's dreaming ability, they have discouraged it until that dream is dormant or even appears dead. Rather than tenderly helping the spouse understand and begin to verbalize their own heart, they power forward leaving their wife/husband drowning in the wake.

The alignment wobbles.

Drawing Out the Vision

A Level 5 marriage has learned how to embolden one another to envision their future. Proverbs 20:5 tells us, "The purposes of a person's heart are deep waters, but one who has insight draws them out." Such a beautiful picture. Your spouse's heart is "deep waters." Their purposes, motives, and dreams are not easily brought to the surface. Through asking the Holy Spirit for discernment and sensitivity; patient and well-timed questions; and praying for and with your mate, you begin to develop insight to help them pull up the sweet water flowing deep within.

One couple we know always sends up warning signs. Deb and I both noticed that anytime we were at dinner with this couple, the wife would quickly defer to her husband. Almost always, she said to her husband, "You just order for me," or "What do you want me to have, dear?" or "I'll have the same as him." Her thoughts, desires, and voice had become so minimized that she didn't even have a vision for evening dinner. She didn't know what she wanted because for so long her husband had told her what she wanted.

On the flipside, after nearly forty years of marriage Deb and I can look at a menu and usually forecast what each other wants. We have both similar and dramatically different taste buds. I crave spicy. Her Norwegian tongue can't handle hot. I know the foods she has a taste for and dreams about (broccoli and coffee ice cream—no, not mixed together!) We have tried dishes all over the world and have listened to each other's responses. At almost every meal, we share a bite of our food saying, "Taste this," "Try this." Likewise, when you help your spouse "try something" they're interested in to see if they might like it, you align your individual visions. If they do, then you help them "fit it on the plate."

One of Deb's favorite questions to me is, "Does this make your heart sing?" She wants to know whether or not something aligns with who God made me and with the desires of my heart. "Are you doing this to please people, to meet their expectations, or is this your passion? If it is, how can I help?"

Goal-Setting the Vision

For many of the past twenty years, Deb and I have used a practical exercise to help us align our individual visions. The exercise follows this general pattern:

1. Designate a time away at the beginning of the year to dream about where you want to be by the end of the year.
2. Identify eight areas for goal setting: spiritual, intellectual, physical, marriage/family, ministry, vocational, social, and financial.
3. Individually spend time alone praying and envisioning what you each want these areas to look like in a year.
4. Come together to discuss and review each other's goals.
5. Encourage one another but also gently question one another: "Is this goal realistic? Is this what you really want? Does this goal seem a little low? I think you can do better at this one."
6. Ask, "How can I help you get there?"
7. Pray with each other about the goals you set and how you'll achieve them.

We've seen how prioritizing this process of goal setting has made a significant impact on how well we do with accomplishing our goals. It has empowered us to be much more effective "vision partners" for one another.

"I've Got Your Back"

Although 1 Samuel 14 isn't a "marriage" passage, it keenly exemplifies this vision alignment of Level 5 marriages. In it, the Philistines and Israelites are at war. While Saul slumbers with his men, his son, Jonathan, has a desire to take out a strategic outpost of the enemy. Jonathan shares this vision with his armor-bearer who courageously embraces Jonathan's vision and declares: "Do all that you have in mind. Go ahead; I am with you heart and soul" (1 Sam. 14:7).

This guy proved it, too. Check out 1 Samuel 14:13: "Jonathan climbed up, using his hands and feet, with his armor-bearer right behind him. The Philistines fell before Jonathan, and his armor-bearer followed and killed behind him."

Recently, we were honored to spend four days in the home of Andrew and Katharine Gardner, pastors of an influential church in Preston, England. We're in a similar stage of life and ministry as the Gardners. This couple is one of our new examples of a Level 5 marriage, especially in the area of vision alignment. We observed them lead their church, conduct a deaf ministry, minister to their Muslim neighbor, mentor pastors, care for two special needs adults, attend their daughter's professional jazz concert, lead us on a four-hour hike through the English hills, spend significant time in prayer with us, and consume gallons of English tea.

One of the most striking facets of their marriage is their support of one another. A few years ago, Katharine felt it was time to fully pursue her longtime vision of being an author. Andrew affirmed her: "Go for it," he said. "I am with you heart and soul." He cheered her forward despite the sacrifice it meant for him and the church. He found creative ways to inspire her. He carved out finances to support the enterprise. He rearranged the house to make a writing space. He commiserated with her when it was tough and rejoiced with her as she moved forward.

While we were there, Katharine Ann Angel's fourth novel arrived from the publishers, and Andrew was bouncing up and down like a kid at Disneyland. Meanwhile, serendipitous and significant ministry doors have opened for Katharine through her new writing. The church is growing too. The Kingdom is advancing.

Everyone needs their spouse to hear their vision and respond, "I am with you heart and soul! Go for it, and I will go with you! I will cover your backside!" The "I can see it with you" affirmation raises and releases all kinds of courage in us.

Marriage Vision Alignment

If you've had a comprehensive eye examination, you know the drill. The optometrist puts the lens apparatus in front of your face and says, "You'll see two of the same letters. Say, "now" as soon as the two letters become one." The test identifies problems in "eye teaming" or binocular vision.

Eye teaming is the ability of both eyes to work together. Each of your eyes sees a slightly different image. Your brain, through a process called fusion, blends these two images into one three-dimensional picture. Good eye coordination keeps the eyes in proper alignment. Deficiency in "eye teaming" is called "convergence insufficiency," which causes blurred or double vision. It's often accompanied by eyestrain, tiredness of the eye, loss of concentration, inefficiency in reading, incoordination, clumsiness, lack of depth perception, and headaches. The interesting fact is that on its own, each single eye has 20/20 vision. But when both eyes are open, you get double vision.

I always thought this particular eye test would be more fun if they used images like eyes, brains or hearts. When the two hearts came together, you could say, "now." When God declares, "the two shall become one," we believe that vision alignment was part of His thinking. We desire for ourselves and other marriages for the two hearts and brains to come together, so we can hear a lot more couples shouting, "Now!"

Most marriages suffer from "convergence insufficiency." Individually, spouses focus on Jesus, ministry, and each other, but they haven't unified their vision. This lack of "vision convergence" results in frequent marriage headaches, tiredness, inefficiency and shallowness. The marriage and the ministry don't go as far as God intends.

What is your unified vision for your marriage? Level 5 marriages have dreamed, prayed, discussed, and planned forward towards God's vision for their marriage. They know what they desire their marriage to look like five, ten, and twenty years from now.

Values to Vision

Healthy vision grows from godly values. Marriage vision begins with essential, agreed-upon values. Determining, stating, and agreeing on these values does not have to be a detailed academic assignment, but it must be meaningful to you.

For example, one of our marriage mantras is, "Pray hard, work hard, play hard!" While this simple value statement doesn't necessarily provide a detailed vision for our marriage, it does state three of our key values, informing and directing our daily decisions together. We start our days with faith-filled praying, then work as hard as we can at our ministry work, and then stop and spend time in play and recreation.

Twenty-five years ago, we decided to place a high value on education and lifelong learning. Since then, we have worked together to finish master's and doctoral degrees. Now, we inform one another's monthly reading lists and continuing education.

Two decades ago, we decided to envision our marriage in decades all the way to 100 years. Deb's Aunt Helga partially inspired this. Aunt Helga is 103 years old but only recently stopped driving to pick up the "old people" for church. We thought, *if we were to both live to be 100, what would we want the main themes for each decade to be?* We dreamed together about what we would want growing old together to look like. We have immense control over some of these visions (like an ever-deepening prayer life together); others, we have no control over (like having grandchildren). Our dreams aren't based on seeing the future, but on knowing our current values.

Starting From the Finish

Stephen Covey, author of *7 Habits of Highly Effective People*, sold millions of books by basically repackaging principles from God's Word. One of his habits is, "Begin with the end in mind."[1] In Bible speak, this equates to, "the fear of the Lord is the beginning of wisdom." Why? Because revering God means we live like God is real, that He has an opinion, and that He will reward or judge at the end. Therefore, live today in light of forever. Vision forces you to visualize the end, and then craft the present in a way that takes you there.

One of the marriage dreams emerging from gazing ahead to year 100 was the goal of snow skiing together in our eighties. Our first date was snow skiing. We have enjoyed it for forty years. We meet couples in their eighties who are still skiing together (admittedly very few!). We realize this dream for the future won't happen by crossing our fingers. We have to work at it now for it to be reality later. We can't guarantee this dream (one of us may die or have our knees give out), but we can increase our chances and significantly influence it.

A Level 5 marriage has excellent "eye-teaming" and "convergence sufficiency." The images of the future have come together into one. No confused or blurred vision!

Ministry Vision Alignment

Level 5 marriages have aligned their vision for their ministry. While each partner has pursued the individual "God dreams" for their lives, together they have also experienced a convergence of their ministry dreams. Their efforts as a team employ the Ecclesiastes 4:9 promise: "Two are better than one because they have a good return for their labor."

CHAPTER 7 | HABIT 5 - VISION ALIGNMENT

In his book, *EntreLeadership*, author Dave Ramsey shares an amazing illustration of synergy:

> "One of the largest, strongest horses in the world is the Belgian draft horse. Competitions are held to see which horse can pull the most, and one Belgian can pull 8,000 pounds. The weird thing is that if you put two Belgian horses in the harness that are strangers to each other, together they can pull 20,000-24,000 pounds. Two can pull not twice as much as one but three times as much as one. This example represents the power of synergy. However, if the two horses are raised and trained together, they learn to pull and think as one. The trained, and therefore unified, pair can pull 30,000-32,000 pounds, almost four times as much as a single horse."[2]

When a husband and wife are teamed together to pull a ministry load, we believe they can accomplish almost three times as much for the Kingdom. If the couple really focuses on working together and trains for it, they can eventually produce four times as much ministry as they could alone.

When Jesus sent His disciples out two by two, He showed us He knew the secret of synergy. He understood the power of two working together toward a common ministry goal. We believe the husband and wife are the "two" Jesus wants to send out. Even if their gifts, personalities, and callings are quite different, the couple can strategize how their ministries can overlap and move them forward to a unified goal.

There really is no exclusive "his" and "hers" in ministry marriages. "Her" ministry is what the husband cares about, wants to see thrive. She gives thought, prayer and work in an effort to see it progress. The same is true for wives towards their husbands' ministry. They are both "ours." But "ours" is even more true when couples harness their gifts together.

The Garden Vision

Deb and I co-pastor together. We talk every day (except on our sabbath) about the church ministry and the shared vision we have for Light & Life church. Yet each of us is uniquely gifted with different passions and callings. When Deb came to me a few years ago to tell me she felt God was opening doors and calling her to plant the first community garden in the home of hip-hop, Compton, California, I was taken aback. Partially because I was scared for her. Our ministry area in North Long Beach is violent enough; our neighboring city of Compton is even worse. A blond, white lady in the garden as drug deals and drive-bys are going down didn't thrill me. I told Deb we really needed to pray about this. It certainly was not my vision.

We prayed. We talked. We envisioned the garden. We discussed how the garden could serve our "together" vision for Light & Life. We examined how I could help and identified realistic expectations. We went to the plot of land and prayed. Sensing God's green light, we launched out together.

The garden is still not "my" thing. Deb has a green thumb; I have a killer thumb (not in a good way). I'm rarely at the garden. But we talk about it almost daily. We pray for it together. I assist her at events and help recruit workers. I take the lead on our church board to acquire funding for it. It is Deb's ministry, but I'm in it with her.

Two years ago, Deb suggested celebrating our family Thanksgiving in the garden. We made a feast and invited the streetwalkers, drug dealers, neighbors, potheads, and the homeless. It was a delightful time of eating and conversation. Six months later, one of the prostitutes who attended came by the garden.

"Pastor Deb, you remember when we had Thanksgiving in the garden?" she asked.

"Yes, Tonya, I certainly do."

"Well", Tonya replied, "that was one of the best days of my life."

Another one of the prostitutes, Tiny, has now received Christ, been baptized, become active in church, and now is helping others get off the street. Other people from the garden have come to our church, and some have met Christ. And folks from our church who have served in the Compton garden have been changed through the experience. Since the garden started, the missional impulse in our church has significantly spiked. Again, the garden is not *my* thing; it's *our* thing. God is honoring our marriage ministry partnership in Compton.

The Level 5 Model Couple

As we said in chapter 2, Aquila and Priscilla could be the designated Level 5 marriage of the New Testament. They are mentioned seven times, and each time their names are found together. Together, they're tentmakers, disciple makers, teachers, evangelists, missionaries, leaders, and church planters. Together, they risked their very lives for the gospel and for Paul (Rom. 16:3,4). All the churches held them in high esteem. They were teamed up, yoked together and had "convergence sufficiency."

One intriguing and culturally disrupting fact about Aquila and Priscilla is the order their names are listed in Scripture references. The ordering of their names varies—two times Aquila is listed first, and five times Priscilla is listed first. To list the wife's name first was highly unusual, yet Priscilla and Aquila were so unified in ministry their names could be flipped—the picture of a marriage oozing with mutual support. Their marriage impacted the New Testament church.

The ministry vision of a marriage will be uniquely shaped by the personality, spiritual gifts, skills, and calling of each individual. Nevertheless, the more unified and mutually supportive a couple is and the greater overlap in ministry values and vision that exists, the more impact the marriage will make for the Kingdom.

Priscilla and Aquila once more underscore the biblical priority of disciple making and multiplying. They were discipled by Paul and became disciplers to Apollos. Then they discipled many from their home. We highlight this because too often, "important" ministry is seen as leadership of a church or a thriving ministry program. Yet the most important work a couple does centers on making disciples who make disciples. Priscilla and Aquila were part of a multiplication discipleship movement. Their influence was monumental, but there's no evidence they ever led anything more than a small group of people in a house church.

One of the key identifiers of a Level 5 marriage is the spiritual maturation past any desire to be heroes. The ego-driven craving to be well known, or to be a hero, has been replaced by the desire to be hero makers. Priscilla and Aquila model this for us with Apollos. They desired to help Apollos learn and grow in wisdom and effectiveness. So they invested heavily in him without thought for themselves. Apollos becomes one of the heroes of the New Testament because the husband-and-wife team obeyed God's calling and mentored him.

Ministry vision in a Level 5 marriage has embraced the multiplication priority of empowering next generations of disciples and leaders. Together, they invest in making disciples who will become disciple makers themselves. While they may lead large or small churches or ministry organizations, their priority is the relational disciple making that creates ongoing chains of multiplying disciples.

The tires on your car don't automatically stay aligned, especially if you're driving through new unpaved territory or hitting potholes, or getting in fender benders with uncaring drivers. It's the same with marriage. Aligning vision is an ongoing process of prayer, faith, heart-sharing and experimentation. But, the more proficient you become at it, the farther you will go and the more fun the journey will be.

Assessment: Aligning Vision

Using the following scales for each question, rate your marriage 1 to 5 on each of these statements:

1. We have conversations about who we want to help each other become.

1	2	3	4	5
Almost Never	Seldom	Frequently	Usually	Almost Always

2. We understand how vision works.

1	2	3	4	5
Not at all	Somewhat	Basically	Fairly Well	Very well

3. We are helping each other advance in the direction of their vision.

1	2	3	4	5
Not at all	Somewhat	Basically	Fairly Well	Very well

4. We have defined key values for our marriage.

1	2	3	4	5
Not at all	Somewhat	Basically	Fairly Well	Very well

5. We have up-to-date goals for the major areas of our lives.

1	2	3	4	5
Not true at all	Somewhat True	Basically True	True	Very True

6. We have clear "joint vision" for how we can minister together.

1	2	3	4	5
Not true at all	Somewhat True	Basically True	True	Very True

7. We invest money and time into improving our marriage and aligning our vision.

1	2	3	4	5
Not true at all	Somewhat True	Basically True	True	Very True

8. We equally value each other's ministry dreams.

1	2	3	4	5
Not true at all	Somewhat True	Basically True	True	Very True

9. We value making disciples who make disciples more than we value growing a bigger ministry.

1	2	3	4	5
Not true at all	Somewhat True	Basically True	True	Very True

10. We mentor other marriages to become more like our marriage.

1	2	3	4	5
Not true at all	Somewhat True	Basically True	True	Very True

CHAPTER 8

By God's Grace for God's Purpose

The Church of Jesus recently said goodbye to one of her stellar leaders—Dave Browning. Dave founded Christ the King Community Church, which went on to plant churches in several states as well as internationally. Dave and his wife, Kristyn, were partners in ministry. In January 2017, Dave was diagnosed with an inoperable brain tumor and told he had three weeks to three months to live. Dave lived courageously for nine months surrounded by family, church and friends.

A few days before his home-going, Kristyn shared a touching and convicting Facebook post: *"A thought on marriage —we are on this earth for a short time. We marry and have kids. We enjoy this life. But I have been thinking about it differently. God gives us a spouse. Together, we are to lead each other toward a relationship with our Creator. Are you encouraging and building up your spouse in their faith? I hope so. I am thankful that God brought Dave and I together. We have weathered many storms together, and I believe we challenged each other in loving God and others."*

Deb and I wept together when we read Kristyn's power-packed words. I jotted down the truth I heard through her words:

- Life is short; we must be urgent about the eternal.
- Life is good; we must taste its joys.

- Our spouses are gifts from God; we must treat them as divine privileges.
- As spouses, we lead each other, evaluating our influence on the other.
- Our ultimate objective is relationship with God; we must not substitute love with works.
- Gratitude for both each other and the gift of marriage is essential.
- Life can be hard; we must weather the storms together.
- Life is about loving God and others; we must inspire one another toward that truth.

More than anything, we hear this widow of a Level 5 marriage saying, "We were together by God's grace for God's purpose, and it was so good."

At our Christian weddings, God does this miracle of "making two become one," but then it's a daily mission to pursue the divine possibilities of this oneness. So few are passionate to have the fullness of God's plan for their marriages. The challenges to marriage are giant, causing most to wander in wilderness circles instead of crossing over into God's promised land.

Marriages need the spirit of Caleb, the Israelite faithful, to declare to each other, "We should go up and take possession of the land, for we can certainly do it" (Num. 13:30). When we do, God unleashes His promises to us, like He did in Caleb's life: "But because my servant Caleb has a different spirit and follows me wholeheartedly, I will bring him into the land he went to, and his descendants will inherit it" (Num. 14:24).

Your marriage can grow to Level 5, but it will mean confronting giants. It won't happen in a single year but Scripture promises us that when we press into God and His power, He'll work in our favor: "Little by little,

I will drive them out before you, until you have increased enough to take possession of the land." (Exodus 23:30).

This "little by little" progress starts with the determination that the promised land is worth the price. Ultimately, you have faith that together with God's power, you can overcome any obstacle and live in His promise. Decision by decision, day by day, week by week, year by year, one battle at a time—working together with God, we further this gradual lifelong progress.

Five Foundational Habits

Your daily habits build the marriage you'll live in, and you can live in either a shack or a mansion. They construct the home your family will grow up in. Throughout this book, we've suggested five foundational habits we believe are essential to growing a Level 5 marriage:

1. **Practicing humility** positions you for an outpouring of God's grace upon you and through you to your spouse. It aligns you with the flow of God's Spirit.
2. **Engaging spiritually** feeds your spirit and marriage with God's presence and truth. Your joint spiritual experiences bind you together in the joy of spiritual intimacy.
3. **Giving honor** identifies and celebrates God's uniqueness in each of you. It invites and empowers your spouse to be all that God has created her/him to be.
4. **Inspiring passion** makes you each other's No. 1 motivator. Practicing this habit picks you up when you're down and instills the drive to zealously advance God's mission.
5. **Aligning vision** focuses your marriage and ministry toward mutually agreed-upon goals. As you team together with a laser focus, you'll go further in fruitfulness for God than you could have ever done alone.

One of the most encouraging meditations for marriage is the promise that *God wants you to have a Level 5 marriage more than you do.* He knows how fulfilling, enjoyable, and productive His gift of marriage can be. He knows how powerfully it can impact your children and forthcoming generations. The question is, "Will we determine to grow forward toward Level 5?"

The marriage vows we make—"For better, for worse, till death do us part"—bring the circumstances life brings and the forthcoming dissolution of our earthly marriage. This vow is noble but reactive to what life throws at you. Perhaps a preceding vow should be, "For your better, even at our worst, 'til our habits of life bring us fully together." Such a vow is proactive, speaking to our daily determination to build our life toward God's dream of oneness. It is a Level 5 marriage vow.

Deb and I love seeing Broadway musicals together. Our favorite is *Wicked*. And we love the song in it, "For Good." We've seen *Wicked* three times, and each time the music starts, we glance at each other and squeeze hands. This song captures our ongoing quest for a Level 5 marriage and our gratitude for what we've already shared. Look at the lyrics below:

> I've heard it said
> That people come into our lives
> For a reason
> Bringing something we must learn
> And we are led to those
> Who help us most to grow
> If we let them
> And we help them in return
> But I don't know if I believe that's true
> But I know I'm who I am today
> Because I knew you . . .

It well may be
That we may never meet again
In this lifetime
So let me say before we part
So much of me
Is made of what I learn from you
You'll be with me
Like a handprint on my heart
And now whatever way our stories end
I know you have rewritten mine
By being my friend . . .
Because I knew you
I have been changed
For good.³

To influence each other for good and for God through the communion of marriage is one of His most splendid gifts—one to be unwrapped and treated with all holiness and reverence.

A Questionable Marriage

If marriage were the primary symbol God selected to reflect the relationship between Jesus and the Church, then we must give our utmost attention to building the marriage God desires. As the world sees this caliber of marriage, they'll be attracted to the source and center of the marriage. They'll see God through our union. Spouses must aspire to, "Live and love so your marriage demands an explanation."

I think of missiologist Michael Frost speaking at a previous Exponential conference a few years ago and exhorting the crowd of church leaders to, "live a questionable life." He challenged his audience to lead the kind of lives people can't help but ask, "What are you about?" Two thousand years ago, the Apostle Peter gave us the same challenge: "But in your hearts, revere Christ as Lord. Always be prepared to give an answer to everyone who asks you to give the reason for the hope that you have. But do this with gentleness and respect" (1 Peter 3:15). Peter assumed that people would be asking questions.

The first prayer Deb and I learned together was taught to us by Lloyd John Ogilvie, who was serving as chaplain for the United States Senate at the time. I'll never forget what he said and how personal it felt: "There was a moment before the world began when God first thought about you, when He first imagined how amazing you could be, when He first sketched you in His mind. We must live into God's dreams about us."

He went on to say that one of the primary ways to live this way was by learning and practicing a simple prayer he had us memorize: "Lord, Make my life as beautiful as it was in Your mind when You first thought about me."

We have spent forty years praying this prayer for ourselves and each other. We have also adapted it to our marriage, praying, "Lord, make our marriage as beautiful as it was in Your mind when You first thought about it." We urge you to pray this for your marriage and see what God will do.

To Fully Flourish

We are still working on our marriage, defending it against the onslaughts of the enemy, exercising mercy in our failures, listening for the unique melody in each other's lives, teaming for the labor of ministry, challenging each other's growth, navigating the aging process together—and through it all having one heck of a time together, laughing our heads off. We're just audacious enough to believe God has put us together for many fantastic reasons, and we want to explore them all. We want to experience what it's like to fully flourish.

Our marriage is still on the potter's wheel. We trust the potter to shape both our marriage and us as individuals so the words of 2 Corinthians 4:7 may ring true: "But we have this treasure in jars of clay to show that this all-surpassing power is from God and not from us."

Our prayer for you is that you would invite the fingers of the potter to work deep into the clay of your marriage. Invite the Holy Spirit to lead you to the Level 5 marriage God designed. The more you grow in this direction, the more the Kingdom will be advanced through your marriage and ministry. We love the dynamic truth that when our marriage flourishes, the Kingdom of God also advances and flourishes.

We pray Ephesians 3:20-21 for you: "Now to him who is able to do immeasurably more than all we ask or imagine, according to his power that is at work within us, to him be glory in the church and in Christ Jesus throughout all generations, forever and ever! Amen."

Endnotes

Introduction

1. *Becoming a Level 5 Multiplying Church* by Todd Wilson and Dave Ferguson with Alan Hirsch (Exponential Resources, 2016).

Chapter 2

1. Transcript from address given at the marriage of HRH Prince William of Wales and Miss Catherine Middleton http://www.westminster-abbey.org/worship/sermons/2011/april/address-given-at-the-marriage-of-hrh-prince-william-of-wales-with-miss-catherine-middleton

2. Ibid.

3. Quote attributed to Susanna Clark and Richard Leigh https://quoteinvestigator.com/2014/02/02/dance/

Chapter 3

1. *Practicing Greatness* by Reggie McNeal and Ken Blanchard (2006, Jossey-Bass), p 10.

2. "What Is Emotional Awareness" by the Korn Ferry Institute https://www.kornferry.com/institute/what-is-emotional-self-awareness

3. "The Magic Relationship Ratio, According to Science" by The Gottman Institute, https://www.gottman.com/blog/the-magic-relationship-ratio-according-science/

4. *Mere Christianity* by C.S. Lewis (Macmillan, 1952).

Chapter 4

1. *The Divine Conspiracy: Rediscovering Our Hidden Life In God* by Dallas Willard (Harper, 1998).
2. *What's Your God Language?* by Gary Thomas (Tyndale Momentum, 2007).

Chapter 5

1. Thomas Merton, *No Man Is an Island* (Mariner Books, 2002).
2. "A Tribute to Lila Mae Trotman," The Navigators, https://www.navigators.org/a-tribute-to-lila-mae-trotman/

Chapter 6

1. *The Notebook* by Nicholas Sparks (Warner Books, 2004).
2. Steve Jobs, commencement address to Stanford University, https://news.stanford.edu/2005/06/14/jobs-061505/
3. *Dead Poets Society*, 2004.

Chapter 7

1. *7 Habits of Highly Effective People* by Stephen Covey (Simon & Schuster Anniversary Edition, 2013.
2. *EntreLeadership* by Dave Ramsey (Howard Books, 2011).
3. "I Have Been Changed for Good," *Wicked*

About the Authors

LARRY WALKEMEYER serves as the Lead Pastor of Light & Life Christian Fellowship in Long Beach, CA. Starting with a handful of committed "white folks," the church has grown into a large multi-ethnic church transforming its tough urban neighborhood. A priority on local and global church planting has led to the start of 22 churches nationally and dozens in Ethiopia, Philippines and Indonesia.

Holding a doctorate in church leadership and the author of eight books, Larry speaks and consults frequently. Larry serves on the Exponential staff as the Director of Equipping and Spiritual Engagement. Azusa Pacific University has recognized Larry with the Centennial Award naming him one of the most influential graduates in its history. Larry serves on the Board of Trustees for Azusa Pacific University.

DEB WALKEMEYER serves as Co-Pastor of Light & Life Christian Fellowship in Long Beach, CA - a large multi-ethnic urban church that has focused on planting churches locally and globally. She also leads the Light & Life Community Center that is assisting in transforming their troubled neighborhood through various initiatives. As a Master Gardener she pioneered and oversees the first Community Garden in Compton, CA where she grows vegetables alongside gang members and prostitutes.

As a licensed Marriage and Family Therapist, Deb has helped many individuals and couples in ministry. She also serves as a regional leader within her denomination. Deb holds five degrees, including a Doctorate in Church Leadership from Fuller Seminary and was recently recognized as one of their outstanding graduates for her years of leadership work in diverse arenas. In addition, she runs a small vacation rental business.

Larry and Deb have been married since 1978. They have two adult daughters. Larry and Deb enjoy snow skiing, waterskiing, biking, traveling, good coffee and long walks on the beach.

www.ingramcontent.com/pod-product-compliance
Lightning Source LLC
Chambersburg PA
CBHW031551040426
42452CB00006B/269